self love for teen girls

AN EMPOWERING GUIDE TO RELEASE AND NURTURE YOUR CONFIDENCE, RESILIENCE, AND EMOTIONAL WELL-BEING WITHOUT THE OVERWHELM

CATHERINE LOUIS

table of contents

This book is dedicated to my 3 teenage granddaughters. May they always realize how unique and talented and loved they are!

introduction

> Love yourself first, and everything else falls in line. You truly have to care for yourself to get things accomplished in this world.
>
> — LUCILLE BALL

Hey, there!

If you're reading this book, chances are that you are wondering what's up with the "self-love" talk? Well, I'm here to tell you that the quote above says it all. You have to love yourself first, because nothing will be truly right in your life if you fail to do this. So, right now, I'd like you to stand in front of a mirror and, say out loud to yourself, "I love myself!", "I can do amazing things!", and "I do not have to be perfect to be loved or to be accepted!" Was that easy… or was it challenging?

I hope that, by the time you finish reading this book and reflecting on the stories, hints, and strategies you will find in this book, that you will be able to stand in front of that mirror with confidence as you tell yourself that you are loved, and you can do amazing things. Let's start with a story.

Imagine you're Sheri, a 15-year-old in high school in Santa Clara County, California. Despite being smart, you're not acing your classes because you're struggling with self-confidence. You often compare yourself to others—how you look, your grades, how popular you are—and it feels like you're always coming up short. Even at home, you feel overshadowed by your older sister, Nicole, thinking your parents favor her over you.

Then, one day, your teacher assigns you to write a letter to yourself, focusing on what makes you unique and what you appreciate about yourself. Working on this assignment, you have a lightbulb moment. You start recognizing your own strengths and achievements that you've been overlooking. This realization sparks a change in how you see yourself. You understand your value, your creativity, determination, and kindness.

Inspired by this new self-awareness, you start a gratitude journal to write down everything you're thankful for. Whenever doubts creep in, you turn to your journal, reminding yourself of your positive qualities and experiences. This practice transforms your mindset. You become more positive, attracting more friends, and gaining respect at school. You even join and excel in the editing club, something you've been passionate about since you were young.

This story of overcoming self-doubt and learning to appreciate oneself speaks to many struggles that teens face, from body image and bullying to peer pressure and family dynamics. It offers hope and practical strategies for building self-esteem and finding one's place. If you're a teenager, a parent, a guardian, or anyone involved in a teen's life, this tale provides valuable insights on navigating adolescence with confidence and grace.

In Chapter 1, you will read about ways to recognize and accept your uniqueness, including your talents and strengths. You will also learn about knowing how to stay away from self-limiting beliefs and understanding how to embrace imperfections. You will also read about practicing self-compassion as well as how to foster a growth mindset. So, let's get started!

CHAPTER 1

discover your strengths and accept yourself

 Different is good. When another person informs you that you are different, smile and keep your head high up with pride.

— ANGELINA JOLIE

Figuring out your self-worth and being cool with who you are is a significant journey. But once you get there, it can lead to incredible achievements and a more satisfying life. First, recognize your strengths (even the hidden ones), and remember it's okay not to be perfect—no one is. Start by noticing all the cool stuff you've done, whether big or small. See every challenge as a chance to learn and become stronger. Hang out with your family and friends and be kind to yourself when things get tough.

To understand your self-worth, you must accept what makes you different. Be true to yourself and don't change just to fit in with others. Find people who share your interests and vibe with you. Be ready to face criticism, but don't let it change what you believe in.

Why is being different so important? Well, being unique lets you do things others can't. And that's true for everyone, making us all special in our own ways. That's how society works—we help each other out. As it is said, "One hand washes the other because a single hand cannot wash itself" (Prasad, 2015). If we were all the same, life would be pretty boring, right? Your uniqueness is what makes you, well, you. Therefore, it is important to realize and identify your talents (Prasad, 2015).

UNCOVER AND APPRECIATE YOUR TALENTS

To discover and nurture your talents, start by reflecting on what you enjoy and are naturally good at. This self-reflection helps you identify your strengths and passions. Which school subjects interest you most? When you dream of a career, what does that look like? Do you have specific activities that make you lose track of time while you are doing them? Is there an activity that makes you reach the flow state—when you get completely absorbed in what you are doing and time seems to stand still? An activity in which you forget about the outside world and perform at the highest level? This is a time to identify your talents.

Is there anything you do that your family seems to appreciate more than others? People often struggle to see their talents; your close friends and family can help you identify them if you struggle to do it yourself. Give them a chance to say what they think about your talents and strengths. Try to be as open to them as possible and consider their feedback.

Look at some areas you are good at but still need some improvement. These are areas you have the potential to excel in. Get rid of all your limiting factors and start believing in yourself. To successfully pursue your dreams, you must first deal with any fear of failure. Do away with negative self-talk and limiting beliefs and have an "I can do it" attitude. Try to understand the root cause of your doubt; then, you can start venturing into new areas where you might find you have talent!

This is the best time in your life to take on challenges and learn new things. Expand beyond your comfort zone and explore a variety of skills to discover which ones you are passionate about. When you have tried different activities, let your heart tell you which ones work best for you. (Mills, 2023).

Imagine you've got a talent, like being really good at softball. It's important to remember that being naturally good at something doesn't mean you'll be the best at it right away. You've got to work at it, practice a lot, and stay determined, even when it gets tough. Just like in video games or any hobby, you don't level up instantly. It takes time, effort, and patience. Don't get bummed out if you don't see big changes fast. Keep your eye on the goal; keep practicing, and you'll see improvement. The key is to keep at it and find chances to do what you love. So, if you love softball, play as much as possible, join a team or play catch with friends. The more you do it, the better you'll get.

PRACTICE SELF-COMPASSION

Self-compassion is like treating yourself as you would treat a good friend who's having a tough time. It's about understanding that everyone messes up sometimes, including you. Think of compassion as being really understanding and caring towards someone who's in trouble. Now, apply that same kindness and understanding to yourself. It's not about being selfish. It's about giving yourself a break and not being too hard on yourself when things don't go right.

For example, if you did something wrong and feel really bad about it, it's easy to get super upset with yourself. But self-compassion means you tell yourself it's okay, learn from it, and move on instead of just feeling terrible. Remember, nobody's perfect, and everyone makes mistakes. Beating yourself up over every little mistake isn't cool or helpful.

There are some easy ways to practice being kind to yourself, like treating yourself with kindness, paying attention to your feelings (that's mindfulness), and remembering that everyone has tough times, not just you. This can help you feel better and handle problems better in the future. We will look at the techniques you can use to practice self-compassion. These techniques include self-kindness, mindfulness, and common humanity (Neff, 2003a; 2003b).

Self-Kindness

Self-kindness, much like self-compassion, can be described as being kind and understanding to yourself when you make a mistake or hurt other people. Instead of blaming and being harsh on yourself, self-kindness will help you see that you shouldn't judge and criticize yourself. You are already in pain, and being hard on yourself may be unfair. It would help if you treated yourself with kindness and warmth. It's time to provide yourself with the care and love you deserve when you face life challenges—and there will be many of them. Be patient and take it easy on yourself when you mess up or don't do things perfectly.

Mindfulness

Mindfulness is like learning to notice your thoughts without getting all worked up about them. It's like saying, "Okay, I'm feeling this way right now," but not letting it take over. Self-compassion is being kind to yourself, especially when you're feeling down or upset. It's about understanding that it's okay to feel bad sometimes and not being too hard on yourself. When something challenging happens, try to keep your cool and handle your emotions without freaking out. Even if you mess up or fail at something important, it's about staying calm and not beating yourself up over it.

Common Humanity

Common humanity is like realizing that messing up is part of being human, and you're not the only one who does it. It's knowing that everyone makes mistakes, and it's okay. You don't have to beat yourself up or feel alone when you slip up. Remember, other people have been there, too, and they've learned to forgive themselves. So, when you make a mistake, don't be too hard on yourself. Instead, be kind and understand that it's just a normal thing that happens to everyone.

FOSTER A GROWTH MINDSET

Teenage brains are not fully developed—they are still going through a process of growth on their way to becoming the brains of an adult. During this period, teenagers experience continuous changes in their emotional behavior; they engage in risky activities and test boundaries (Kiusalaas, 2018). As a teenager, you likely don't want anything to do with how you behaved before you reached this age. As a teenager, you're probably starting to think a lot about your life and how to handle your problems. To develop a growth mindset, which means believing you can improve and grow with effort, here's what you can do:

- **Look for places where you can get inspiring news.** You can find helpful information and inspiring news from sites that provide encouraging content. *Reasons to Be Cheerful* is one such site; Pinterest is also a great place to look for things that can make you happy.

- **Get a chance to feel your emotions.** It's okay if you need time to feel your emotions. If that means crying, then go ahead and cry. This can provide relief and reduce some of your overwhelming emotions.
- **Get Active:** Try some exercise like jogging, walking, or yoga. It helps your brain feel good and lowers stress.
- **Remember Your Tough Times:** Think about times you've gotten through hard stuff before. Remembering this can help you feel strong again.
- **Talk to Someone You Trust:** Share what's bothering you with someone like your parents, a friend, or a mentor. Talking can make problems feel smaller and more apparent.
- **Take a Break:** If school's tough with bad grades or friend issues, take a day off to clear your head. Sometimes, stepping back helps you see things differently.
- **Think of Someone Strong:** Know someone who's really tough? Keep them in mind when you're feeling down. It can inspire you to be strong, too.
- **Meditate:** Spend some quiet time focusing on what you want. It's an excellent way to calm down and feel grounded.
- **Take a walk in Nature:** Feeling down? Go for a walk outside. It's refreshing and can help you think better.
- **Write in a Journal:** Write down your thoughts and what happens in your day. It's a great way to understand your challenges and learn from them. Keeping a journal will help you understand that some of the challenges you face are actually opportunities for learning new things and growing.

- **Help Others Be Strong:** If you help a friend be resilient, it can boost your own strength, too. Giving support to someone close to you—helping them improve their resilience—can also assist you in raising your own resilience (Waters, 2013).

Remember, developing a growth mindset is about believing in your potential and working towards it, no matter the challenges.

OVERCOME SELF-DOUBT AND BUILD SELF-ESTEEM

Self-doubt means you lack confidence and are unsure of your capabilities. Individuals with self-doubt are hard on themselves—they believe they are short of something they should have but don't. To overcome this self-doubt, you have to replace it with self-esteem. Self-esteem refers to feeling appreciated and liked. Teens can replace self-doubt with self-esteem.

Your self-esteem, or how you feel about yourself, can really be influenced by the people around you, like your friends, family, and teachers. When these people in your life focus on the good stuff about you and accept you for who you are, it makes you feel more confident and prouder. They play a huge part in either boosting your self-esteem or bringing it down. If you're always getting criticized or told off more than you're praised, it can make you feel low about yourself. Also, being made fun of or bullied by friends or siblings can really hurt how you see yourself. The way others treat you and talk to you can have a big impact on your self-esteem. When you always receive harsh words and poor treatment, it will affect how you think about yourself (Nemours TeensHealth, 2023).

Learn how to deal with the voice in the back of your head. Try to stop that negative voice from saying bad things about yourself, such as *I don't think I will ever be able to make it in life!* or *My school grades will never improve!* Such negative thoughts will hurt your self-esteem and cause you to doubt yourself. Here are some more tips on how you can overcome self-doubt and build self-esteem:

· **Surround yourself with people who are supportive and treat you well.** Avoid individuals who like to pull you down- by their actions or what they say. You will feel good when you are with people who accept you the way you are and do not judge you. Of course, you have to also treat them with the same love and respect.

- **Say to yourself only things that can help you.** Your self-esteem, or how you feel about yourself, can really be influenced by the people around you, like your friends, family, and teachers. When these people in your life focus on the good stuff about you and accept you for who you are, it makes you feel more confident and prouder. They play a huge part in either boosting your self-esteem or bringing it down. If you're always getting criticized or told off more than you're praised, it can make you feel pretty low about yourself. Also, being made fun of or bullied by friends or siblings can really hurt how you see yourself. How others treat you and talk to you can greatly impact your self-esteem.
- **Remind yourself that, like everyone else, you are not perfect.** Try to do your best, and feel proud of yourself. Anyone can make mistakes; if you do, accept them, forgive yourself, and move on.
- **Set goals for yourself and work toward achieving them.** Reasonable goals would be to study harder or start a healthy eating plan. So, make a plan and then work to accomplish it. Make a follow-up list and track your progress—any progress you have made—and then remember to be proud of yourself.

- **Concentrate more on what is going well.** Avoid seeing only what is wrong or bad. Learn to have a balance of seeing good and what is wrong, but don't dwell on the wrong. Learn to bounce back from your mistakes; focus on what you are doing well. Instead of letting your mind go through what went wrong during the day, throw those negative thoughts away and replace them with the good that happened instead. At the end of each day, think about three things that went well and feel happy about them (Nemours TeensHealth, 2023). This is how you learn to notice good things in your life.

THE STORY OF AGANETHA

Aganetha was a 17-year-old with lots of confidence. She was almost done with high school and clear about her goals and what she didn't want in life. She felt pretty good about herself, rating her self-esteem 8 out of 10. But she sometimes got stuck on negative thoughts, like focusing on her hairy legs when someone complimented her figure. She knew these negative "yeah, buts" were holding her back from feeling even better about herself.

Despite having a family with some anger issues, Aganetha managed to stay positive, thanks to supportive friends. She was strong-minded, especially around boys. She once ended a short relationship because the guy tried to pressure her into things she wasn't comfortable with. Aganetha believed in respecting her own values and boundaries, especially in relationships.

She worked hard to improve her self-esteem even more. She hung out with friends who boosted her up and made her see her own strengths. Aganetha also focused on personal growth and self-care, doing things that made her happy and following her interests to build more skills and confidence.

Her strong self-esteem protected her from negativity and led her to healthy relationships. She knew the importance of being with people who respected her for who she was. Throughout her life, her self-esteem was like a guiding star, helping her make decisions that respected her values and supported her well-being. Aganetha became a role model for others, showing the power of knowing your worth and living true to yourself.

COMING UP

Okay, so you've learned some cool ways to discover your talents. Now, it's time to put those ideas into action. You've got the info on how to appreciate what makes you unique and be cool with who you are. You've also figured out how to get past those doubts that hold you back and be kinder to yourself. Plus, you learned about having a growth mindset, which means believing you can get better at things. Next up, in Chapter 2, we will talk about building rock-solid confidence and discovering what you're passionate about. Let's jump into Chapter 2 and see what awesome stuff we can learn!

build unshakable confidence—uncover your strengths and capabilities

Calm mind brings inner strength and self-confidence, so that's very important for good health.

— DALAI LAMA

The Dalai Lama's advice is really timeless and super relevant, especially for teen girls who are figuring out who they are and growing into themselves. Consider this chapter an exciting journey to boost your confidence and tap into what you're capable of, especially for teen girls, figuring out who they are and what they want from life. First, we will dig into your hobbies and interests to help you find hidden talents and spark a fire inside you. By aligning what you dream about with what you do, you start to walk a path that's true to you, which lights up your confidence.

But hey, it's normal to bump into fear and self-doubt. We have some cool tricks to help you beat those doubts, shake off the negative thoughts, and see failure as a step towards growing and improving. You'll find ways to bounce back from tough times and discover the real strength you have inside.

Confidence isn't just about what you achieve alone. It's also about how you act with others. We'll explore how to show confidence when you're with people, whether they're friends, family, or even at school. You'll learn about talking confidently, setting clear boundaries, and standing up for yourself in a way that's true to who you are. This helps build relationships that lift you up and support your goals. (Jacobson, 2017).

So, take a deep breath, keep an open mind, and let your heart be at ease. As you read on, you'll discover how to build rock-solid confidence, discover your strengths, and embrace all the incredible potential you've got inside, ready to shine.

UNLEASH THE POWER WITHIN: DISCOVER AND PURSUE TEENAGE PASSIONS

Being a teenager is all about exploring, being curious, and finding out who you are. It's a time when you start to figure out what you're really passionate about, those things that really get you excited and make you feel alive. Let's dive into this adventure of discovering what you love, using your talents, and growing your confidence.

First off, trying different things is key. Get involved in various activities to see what you enjoy most. You might find your passion in helping the environment, writing stories for the school magazine, or something entirely different. It's all about exploring and seeing what clicks with you.

Once you find something you love, it's time to get really good at it. This might mean taking classes, finding a mentor, or just practicing a lot. For example, if you're into photography, you could spend hours learning about it, experimenting with different techniques, and taking awesome photos. The better you get, the more confident you'll feel in your abilities.

Chasing your passions also means facing challenges and learning from them. Every obstacle is a chance to grow stronger and more resilient. Think about a singer who keeps attending auditions and competitions, even when it's tough. Her determination helps her perform on bigger stages and inspire others.

Your teenage years consist of a period in which you brim with exploration, curiosity, and self-discovery. This is when you transform and begin the mission to discover your passions, those underlying sparks that light up your soul and set it on fire (Jacobson, 2017). Let's go deep into the journey of discovering passion, talent utilization, and confidence development that clears the way for you to release your real potential.

Investigating interests and establishing personal passions is an important first step. By involving yourself in a wide spectrum of activities, you can learn key perspectives into what really thrills your heart and mind. Whether it's in voluntary work, joining groups of like-minded people, or experimenting with various hobbies, the exploration phase allows you to test different dimensions of life. For example, you may develop a passion for environmental causes through engaging in a beach cleanup or seek fun through writing by contributing your stories to a school magazine.

Creating skills and furthering competence in things of interest is the bridge that links passion to mastery (Jacobson, 2017). Once a passion is established, you can dig deeper, utilizing time and effort to obtain information and improve your potential. You might have to enroll in courses, look for mentorship, or engage in consistent activities to enhance your skills. Imagine yourself being obsessed with photography and being able to dedicate hours to studying composition skills, toying around with various lenses, and capturing thrilling images. As your skills grow, so will your confidence in your capacity to exhibit yourself through your art.

Developing confidence by chasing passions is a life-changing process. As you take part in activities that resonate with your passions, you are exposed to problems and drawbacks that test your resolve; however, each challenge creates a chance for growth (Jacobson, 2017). By remaining dedicated and relentlessly driving forward, you cultivate resilience, self-belief, and a never-say-die attitude. A good example is a young dancer who takes part in auditions and competitions. She experiences periods of self-doubt but is relentless in pursuit of her passion, ultimately performing on bigger platforms and positively influencing others with her elegance and confidence.

We can find a wealth of inspiration in studying the motivational journeys of some teenage girls who went after their passions. Take, for example, Gitanjali Rao, a young inventor who is crazy about applying science to handle real-world challenges. Her commitment made her the first Kid of the Year recognized by *TIME* magazine. In her own words, Gitanjali said, "Never allow age to shape your potential. Passion has no limits for those who believe in themselves."

As you walk on your individual path to discover passion, you must learn to explore, establish skills, and develop confidence. Embrace the distinct journey before you; inside, it can power your real potential. Let the words of influential Gitanjali echo within your heart: "Have faith in your passions, believe in your potential, and look on as your confidence reaches new levels, lighting the path for your dreams to turn into reality."

As you find your passions, develop skills, and build confidence, remember this journey is unique. It's about believing in what you love, seeing your potential grow, and turning your dreams into reality. Embrace this journey, and you'll discover more about who you are and what you can do.

CONQUER SELF-DOUBT AND FEAR: EMBRACE YOUR INNER COURAGE

As a teenager, you might find self-doubt and fear creeping in, making it challenging to grow and chase what you love. But with the right mindset and strategies, you can beat these challenges and unlock your courage to seize new opportunities.

Fighting off negative thoughts about yourself is vital to beating self-doubt. Whenever you catch yourself thinking something negative, like "I'm terrible at math," try flipping it to something positive, like "I can get better at math with practice." This helps change your mindset.

Stepping out of your comfort zone is also crucial. Handling fear and leaving your comfort zone is important for personal development (Harris, 2022). Start with small steps, like trying a new activity or speaking in front of classmates. Feeling a bit scared is okay, but pushing through can help you discover hidden strengths. Imagine joining a debate club to overcome a fear of public speaking and becoming a confident speaker.

Positive affirmations and visualization can really boost your mindset. By repeating positive phrases such as, "I am deserving, I am capable, and I am enough," you can combat self-doubt and develop a powerful sense of self-trust. Also, try picturing yourself succeeding in your mind, a technique even top athletes use to prepare for big events.

Remember, overcoming fear and self-doubt is part of growing up. Nelson Mandela said it best: "Courage is not the absence of fear, but the triumph over it." Facing these challenges head-on helps you realize your true potential and change your life for the better.

Before we end this section, I would like to share two inspiring, real-life stories of girls who conquered self-doubt and found success, beginning with the story of Malala Yousafzai.

Malala Yousafzai from Pakistan is a fantastic example of beating self-doubt and making a big difference. Growing up in Swat Valley, she bravely stood up for girls' right to learn, even when the Taliban tried to scare her. When she was just 15, a Taliban member shot her in the head on her way to school. Miraculously, she survived, which only made her stronger and more determined. Instead of giving in to fear, she became a powerful voice for girls' education all around the world. Her hard work and courage paid off big time when she won the Nobel Peace Prize at only 17, becoming the youngest person ever to receive this honor. Malala continues her fight for education and equality for girls everywhere with her Malala Fund, inspiring young people to overcome their doubts and chase their dreams.

Serena Williams is one of the most amazing tennis players ever. She's faced a ton of challenges, including doubting herself and dealing with unfair treatment because of her gender and race. Growing up in Compton, California, she and her family didn't have much money, making chasing her dream of playing tennis professionally extremely tough. But Serena's incredible talent and hard work helped her rise to the top. She's won 23 Grand Slam singles titles, more than any other tennis player in recent times. Serena is a true legend, not just for her wins but for showing her determination, passion, and ability to bounce back. She's been open about her struggles, like feeling unsure about her body, being a mom while playing top-level tennis, and overcoming self-doubt. Her story is super inspiring, showing girls and women everywhere that they can overcome doubts and achieve their dreams, no matter what field they're in. Serena proves you can do amazing things if you believe in yourself and keep pushing through tough times.

Finally, building confidence in your interactions and creating solid relationships is important. Speak your mind confidently, set clear boundaries, and surround yourself with supportive people. This helps you grow emotionally and establish lasting, positive relationships.

RADIATE CONFIDENCE IN RELATIONSHIPS

Imagine being a teen who's super good at showing confidence in relationships by developing healthy limits, fostering supportive friendships, and talking things out well. (Harris, 2022). That can make your friendships strong and help you grow as a person.

Now, let's talk about Lorna from Nashville. She felt out of place, unsure of herself because she didn't fit society's idea of success and beauty. But deep down, Lorna knew she was more than what people saw.

Lorna decided to accept herself just as she was. She started to follow her dreams, using art and dance to show her authentic self. Sure, some people doubted her because she wasn't following the usual path, but Lorna didn't let that stop her. She found friends who really got her and helped her see her true worth.

As she grew up, Lorna's confidence started to blossom. She learned to ignore the negative voices and celebrate even her smallest wins. She realized that accepting yourself is a never-ending adventure.

Lorna's genuine vibe attracted others who were also trying to find themselves. They formed a community that valued being different and supported each other's unique paths.

Lorna's journey taught her the importance of loving and accepting yourself. She found happiness in being true to who she was. As she went through life, she inspired other girls, showing them that they, too, could embrace who they are and start their own incredible journeys to self-acceptance.

COMING UP

Building strong confidence and knowing your power and potential is a big deal. It's all about understanding yourself, being okay with who you are, and taking steps to grow. Here's a quick rundown of what we've learned about boosting confidence:

- **Self-Reflection:** It's important to think about what you believe in, what you value, and what you aim for. This helps you to be your true self when you do stuff. Knowing what you're good at and what you've achieved before helps you feel more confident.
- **Self-Acceptance:** You've got to be cool with your mistakes and things you're not so good at. Everyone messes up sometimes, and that's okay. Learning to be kind to yourself, even when you goof up, is a big step in building confidence.
- **Positive Self-Talk and Affirmations:** The way you talk to yourself matters. Choosing words that lift you up boosts your belief in what you can do.
- **Take Action:** Set goals you can reach, be proud of small wins, do not give up when things get tough. These help build a strong, confident mindset.

- **Lifelong Process:** Confidence-building doesn't happen overnight. It takes continuous effort and self-kindness. The more you practice these things, the more confident you'll become.

In the next chapter, we'll dive into how to deal with stress and create a balanced life. You'll learn how to face challenges head-on, live a healthier life, and use nifty strategies to cope with stress, making you stronger and more balanced.

CHAPTER 3

manage stress and overwhelm— find your balance

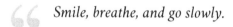

66 *Smile, breathe, and go slowly.*

—THICH NHAT HANH

L ife as a teenager can be wild and full of stuff to juggle, from school stress to social drama and everything in between. It can get pretty overwhelming, right? Well, it's important to know that you're not alone in feeling this way. Did you know that a whopping 80% of girls your age deal with regular stress, and 1 out of 3 of us even feel super overwhelmed to the point of burnout? Yeah, it's a big deal, but don't worry, we've got your back! In this chapter, we're diving into how to handle stress like a boss and create a balanced life.

Let's start by talking about why this is such a big deal. The stats might sound scary, but they show us that we've got to take stress seriously. We're going to chat about self-care stuff like exercising, sleeping enough, and eating well to keep our energy up and stay healthy. Plus, we'll spill the tea on mindfulness and relaxation techniques to help us find peace amid all the craziness.

But here's the secret ingredient: building a support squad! We'll share how important it is to talk openly with trusted adults and make strong friendships that have our backs. By using these tricks, you'll be able to tackle stress head-on and create a life that's chill and fulfilling, even when the world feels like a rollercoaster.

Let's get into it! To stay on top of stress, we will explore self-care stuff like keeping a solid sleep schedule, staying active, and eating healthy. Plus, we'll talk about time management, setting boundaries, and making sure we have time for the things that make us happy.

We'll also share some handy stress-busting tips like mindfulness, deep breathing, and being thankful for what we have. Building a squad of supportive people is a big deal, too, so we'll chat about keeping it real with adults you trust and finding friends who've got your back. Having people to talk to and lean on can make all the difference.

UNDERSTAND STRESS AND WHAT IT DOES

You've probably noticed that being a teenager can be super stressful. We get it! You've got school stuff, social stuff, and life stuff to deal with. Stress is like your body's way of saying, "Whoa, slow down, girl!" It's totally normal, but it can mess with your head and body if you don't deal with it right.

Here's the deal: stress is just your body's reaction to all the stuff happening around you. It's your brain's way of saying, "Hey, this is a lot to handle!" So, it's important to know what's stressing you out. It could be homework, friends, or family stuff. When you know what's bugging you, you can start to do something about it.

Understanding stress is like knowing your enemy. Most of us can tell when stress is creeping into our lives. We know that school, friends, and other things can get us worked up. Think about it – preparing for exams, dealing with friendship drama, or handling extracurricular stuff can make our stress levels go through the roof.

But here's the cool part: once you know what's stressing you out, you can start to deal with it. For example, if you know that social media is a big source of stress, you can limit your time on it and do stuff that helps you chill instead. And don't forget, stress can mess with your body too, like messing up your sleep, making it hard to focus, or even causing physical problems like headaches or tummy trouble. But if you know this, you can focus on taking care of yourself and handle stress like a champ!

To keep stress from taking over, we've got a bunch of tricks to share with you. We're talking about stuff like mindfulness, deep breathing, and finding things to be thankful for. And don't forget about your support squad – having people to talk to and get advice from is a game-changer.

Find Your Stress Triggers

Now, let's talk about something super important: knowing what makes you stressed. Every girl is different, and what bugs you might not bother someone else. It's like having your own personal stress triggers. Once you know what yours are, you can start figuring out how to deal with them.

So, think about what makes you stressed. Is it schoolwork, family stuff, or drama with friends? Once you pinpoint what's bugging you, you're on your way to handling it better. For example, if you know that tests stress you out, you can break studying into smaller chunks so it's not so overwhelming. And remember, it's okay to ask for help or take a breather when you need it. Be kind to yourself!

Once you've got a handle on your stress triggers, it's time to come up with some self-care strategies. These are things you can do to take care of your mental and physical well-being. It's like giving yourself a little TLC.

You might find that exercise, journaling, or talking to a friend helps you relax and feel better. And don't forget to be kind to yourself – it's totally okay to take a break and ask for help when you need it. By practicing self-care and being gentle with yourself, you'll become a stress-busting superstar!

So, here's the scoop: we all have our own stress triggers, stuff that gets us worked up. It could be school stuff, family stuff, or whatever. Once you figure out what's stressing you out, you can start to deal with it. Remember to be your own best friend.

RELAX AND FIND PEACE

Now, let's talk about some cool ways to keep your stress levels in check. One secret weapon is mindfulness – it's all about being in the moment and paying attention to your thoughts and feelings without judging yourself. Mindfulness can help you lower stress, focus better, and just feel happier.

One way to practice mindfulness is through deep breathing exercises and guided meditation. These are like superpower tools for calming your mind. By taking a few minutes each day to breathe deeply or do a quick meditation, you can find your inner zen and keep stress at bay.

Don't forget about relaxation techniques. These are all about giving yourself a break. You can take warm baths, do yoga, or listen to your fave tunes to unwind. It's all about finding what helps you chill and making it part of your routine. You deserve it!

It's also a great idea to talk to your support squad about mindfulness. Sharing your journey with trusted adults and friends can be super helpful. They can give you tips, and you can all learn and grow together.

SET BOUNDARIES AND MANAGE YOUR TIME FOR SUCCESS

Alright, now let's tackle time management and setting boundaries. These skills are like your keys to success! You'll learn how to prioritize tasks, use your time wisely, and say no when you need to. This will help you ace your schoolwork, follow your passions, maintain healthy relationships, and enjoy the good stuff in life.

First up, time management. It's all about making a schedule that works for you. You can jot down your school stuff, extracurriculars, and anything you want to do for fun. This way, you can see your time and plan it out like a boss.

Next, learn to prioritize. Figure out what's super important and tackle those tasks first. This way, you'll get the big stuff done before moving on to the less important things.

Break tasks into smaller bits to avoid getting overwhelmed. Big projects can be scary, but if you divide them into smaller tasks, you'll make progress and not procrastinate.

And please, please, please avoid multitasking! It might seem like a good idea, but it can actually make you less productive. Focus on one thing at a time, finish it, and then move on to the next.

Now, let's chat about setting boundaries with technology and social media. We all love our devices, but sometimes, they can take over our lives. So, set some rules like having tech-free zones or times. For example, no phones during meals or before bedtime.

Limit your social media time, too. It's easy to get lost scrolling endlessly, so use apps that track and limit your time on social media.

And those notifications? They can be super distracting, so consider turning off nonessential ones when you're studying or doing important stuff to stay focused and get more done.

Lastly, remember to make time for self-care and relaxation. Schedule activities that make you happy, like exercising, reading, or just chilling with loved ones. It's essential to take care of yourself and put your mental and physical health first.

Remember, these skills are like your ticket to success, and they'll come in handy even when you're not a teenager anymore. So, start practicing now, and you'll be a superstar at balancing your life.

THE STORY OF BELLA HOLDEN

Let's take a moment to talk about Bella Holden. She was like a force of nature in sunny Arizona, full of determination and energy, ready to conquer the world. But beneath her vibrant exterior, she was facing a silent battle. Bella was caught up in the relentless stress that affects many teenage girls today.

As a junior in high school, Bella was drowning in academic pressure and extracurricular commitments. She was determined to secure a spot at a prestigious university, but this pursuit pushed her to the brink. Her days were a whirlwind of AP classes, sports practices, and college prep courses.

Sleep became a distant dream for Bella. She spent her nights cramming for exams or perfecting college essays, leaving no time for rest. The weight of expectations bore down on her, robbing her of the much-needed relaxation.

Physically, Bella's body rebelled against the constant stress. Her once-boundless energy faded, replaced by persistent fatigue. Headaches became a constant companion, a reminder of the mounting pressure. Even her immune system gave in, and she found herself getting sick more often.

Amidst this chaos, Bella's social life suffered. Friendships crumbled under the weight of her packed schedule, leaving her feeling lonely. She yearned for companionship but felt trapped in a cycle of obligations.

Thankfully, Bella's story took a positive turn. Recognizing the toll that stress was taking on her, she sought help from supportive teachers and her loving family. They encouraged her to prioritize self-care and carve out moments of peace. They reminded her that her worth wasn't solely based on her achievements but also on her happiness and well-being.

With their support, Bella began a journey of self-discovery. She learned to set boundaries, say no when needed, and explore mindfulness techniques. Slowly but surely, she regained her autonomy and learned to navigate her stress.

Bella's story serves as a powerful reminder of the challenges faced by teenage girls like her. It highlights the urgent need for society to prioritize mental health and well-being, offering support and resources to help these young warriors fight their silent battles. Let's stand together, offering understanding, compassion, and the tools to sail through the stormy seas of adolescence.

COMING UP

In this chapter, we dove into the world of managing stress and overwhelm as teen girls. We've talked about the things that stress us out, like school pressure, social expectations, and the never-ending presence of technology. We've also explored how chronic stress can mess with our bodies and minds, stressing the importance of balance and self-care.

So, what is the key takeaway from this chapter? Managing stress and overwhelm is crucial for keeping our lives in harmony. By practicing self-care and using healthy coping strategies, we equip ourselves with the tools to face challenges head-on and improve our overall well-being.

In Chapter 4, we'll delve into the topic of embracing positive body image and celebrating the beauty of diversity. In today's world, girls often face unrealistic beauty standards that can make us feel inadequate. We'll shine a light on how media and societal pressures impact our self-image and encourage you to love and appreciate your unique body, knowing that beauty comes in all shapes, sizes, and colors. By embracing positive body image and celebrating diversity, you'll boost your self-worth and confidence, fostering your mental and emotional well-being.

celebrate body diversity

"YOUR BODY IS A PIECE OF ART, EMBRACE IT WITH LOVE AND CARE.

 It's the only one you have, and it's unique.

— UNKNOWN

Ever thought about why we all seem to chase after the "perfect" body, pushed on us by everything from billboards to our Insta feeds, instead of just loving the variety of people out there? This chapter dives into the super important topic of feeling good about your own body and why it's awesome to celebrate everyone's uniqueness.

Society's got us chasing impossible beauty standards with all those pics of perfect, photoshopped bodies everywhere. This constant pressure leads to a bunch of us feeling down about how we look, not being happy with our bodies and sometimes even picking up bad habits to try and fit into these narrow beauty ideals. It's about time we start questioning these fake standards and get hyped about how different and cool we all are.

We're going to take a close look at how ads, movies, and even the culture around us mess with how we see ourselves, pushing this idea that there's only one way to be "beautiful." By thinking about how all this affects us, we can start fighting back against these harmful ideas and feel better about ourselves.

At the heart of feeling great about how you look is getting that everyone's different, and that's what makes us all special. We'll share some stories and examples that show how important it is to include everyone and see beauty in all shapes and sizes. By learning to love your own body and not waste time comparing yourself to others, you can start feeling more confident and focus on what really matters—like being healthy and happy and doing things that make you feel good.

So, let's ditch those unrealistic beauty goals and start celebrating what makes each of us unique. With some self-love, a bit of mindfulness, and support from friends and family, you can discover how to be happy with yourself just the way you are.

CHALLENGE UNREALISTIC BEAUTY STANDARDS AND MEDIA MESSAGES

In the world we're living in, stuffed with Instagram feeds and magazine covers, it feels like there's a lot of pressure on how we should look, especially for teens. It's like everywhere you look, there's this picture-perfect image of what beauty's supposed to be, but guess what? A lot of it isn't even real. It's all about challenging these impossible standards that the media throws at us.

So, how do you fight back? Start by getting objective with what you see online and in magazines. Know that many of those "flawless" images are super edited and don't show the incredible variety of real people out there. It's about seeing through the fakes and loving the real you.

You've got the power to change the game. Support and follow people and brands that celebrate all kinds of beauty – different shapes, colors, and sizes. It's about making noise for what's real and pushing back against those old-school beauty "rules."

Social media's a tricky thing, right? It can make you feel down when you're scrolling and comparing yourself to others. But here's the deal: you control your feed. Fill it with positive vibes and people who lift you up, not tear you down. And remember, it's okay to take a break from the screen to take care of yourself.

Building up your self-esteem is critical. Remind yourself that you're more than just a selfie. You've got talents, dreams, and a whole lot of stuff that makes you, well, you. Celebrating that is what real beauty is about.

Tackling beauty standards is more than just a one-person job. It's about all of us getting smarter about what we see, sharing the real deal, and supporting each other. By doing this, we're not just changing how we see beauty but also setting the stage for everyone to feel great about being themselves. Let's make it happen!

TAKE CARE OF YOURSELF AND BE GRATEFUL

Taking care of both your mind and body is essential for feeling good about yourself. This means doing things like working out, eating foods that make you feel great, and getting enough z's. Also, chill time is necessary – whether meditating, writing down your thoughts, or just hanging out in nature.

Loving and accepting your body for what it is is a big part of self-care. It's all about celebrating what makes you unique and focusing on your strengths rather than getting hung up on looks. Positive vibes and kicking negative thoughts to the curb can boost how you see yourself.

For all the girls out there, it's time to shake up those old beauty standards. Beauty's not one-size-fits-all – it's every shape, color, and size. Ditch the comparison game and cheer on everyone's unique look. Supporting brands and people who get this and pushing for all kinds of beauty in the media is how we start changing the game.

Self-care isn't just a buzzword – it's about building your confidence and rocking who you are. By sticking to a self-care plan, loving your body, and celebrating everyone's different looks, you're not just helping yourself; you're encouraging others to feel fabulous, too. So, let's make feeling good about ourselves a top priority and show the world the real meaning of beauty.

DEVELOP A HEALTHY RELATIONSHIP WITH FOOD

Creating a healthy lifestyle is about balance, not cutting out entire food groups or pushing yourself too hard at the gym. It's about filling your plate with a mix of fruits, veggies, whole grains, proteins, and fats that make you feel good. And when it comes to staying active, pick activities you enjoy instead of just working out to look a certain way.

It's essential to watch for signs that your eating habits might be going off track, like if you're not eating enough, eating way too much in one go, or can't stop thinking about your weight and food. If you notice this happening, it's a good idea to talk to someone you trust—like a family member, teacher, or doctor. Learning about the risks of eating disorders and being in a space where everyone's relaxed about discussing body image can really help catch problems early.

Developing a chill attitude towards eating means listening to your body's hunger signals, enjoying your food without guilt, and ditching the labels of "good" or "bad" food. Embracing every meal with a positive vibe and knowing it's okay to treat yourself is critical. Plus, it's about seeing your body in a positive light, valuing it for what it can do, not just how it looks.

For teen girls, getting these habits down can lay the groundwork for feeling great about yourself and your food choices for life. By focusing on balanced eating, understanding and addressing any food issues, and loving your body for its awesomeness, you're setting yourself up for a happier, healthier you.

SARAH AND EMILY'S JOURNEY

In a cozy spot in their high school's cafeteria in New Jersey, two friends, Sarah and Emily, would often chat about the tough time they were having with their body image. They were really hard on themselves, trying to match the impossible beauty standards they saw all over the media, which led them down some unhealthy paths.

One day, while venting about all this, Sarah came across a quote that hit home: "Beauty isn't about what you see in the mirror; it's about the kindness in your heart and the strength of your spirit." This quote struck a chord with both of them, sparking a sense of self-acceptance and a drive to break away from society's narrow view of beauty.

Together, they started a journey of self-discovery. They reached out to people who could guide them and learned more about how to eat right—not as a way to punish themselves but to fuel their bodies. They also found fun ways to stay active that made them feel good, rather than exercising just to look a certain way.

Bit by bit, Sarah and Emily managed to let go of their body image issues. They stopped seeking approval from others and started appreciating and loving themselves. They found a community that celebrated everyone's uniqueness and encouraged body positivity.

As they grew more confident, Sarah and Emily started to spread the word about the importance of a healthy body image and eating well. They wanted everyone to know that true beauty comes from being yourself and caring for your body and mind. Their story inspired others who were struggling, showing them that it's totally possible to let go of societal expectations and embrace a healthier, self-accepting approach to life.

Their journey reminds us all that true self-acceptance and a positive relationship with food come from kindness toward ourselves, determination, and the belief that beauty is much more than appearance.

COMING UP

Wrapping up this chapter, we're moving past the toxic chase for a so-called perfect body and welcoming the power of diversity with open arms. By learning to see the beauty in yourself as you are, you're not just changing your life but also making our world more accepting and kind. It's about time we celebrate everyone's unique beauty, no matter their size, shape, or look, and work towards a future where every kind of beauty is valued.

The media has a massive role in how we see beauty, bombarding us with perfect, photoshopped images everywhere we look. But now that we know how damaging these fake standards can be, we can start loving ourselves for who we are.

Thinking about what you've learned from this chapter, ask yourself:

How has this changed my view on body image influenced by society?

Do I feel more ready to stand up against these unrealistic beauty standards and appreciate all kinds of beauty?

How can I spread this positive vibe to help others feel good about themselves, too?

As we close this chapter on body positivity and the celebration of diversity, we're about to dive into Chapter 5. In today's world, where we're always online, looking after our mental health is crucial. This next chapter will explore how too much screen time affects us, why setting some screen limits is important, and how creating healthy habits can boost our mental well-being.

create balance in a hyperconnected world

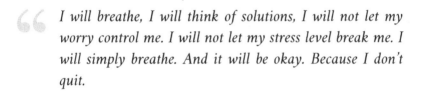

> *I will breathe, I will think of solutions, I will not let my worry control me. I will not let my stress level break me. I will simply breathe. And it will be okay. Because I don't quit.*

— SHAYNE MCCLENDON

Ever noticed how glued we are to our screens and what that's doing to our heads? This chapter dives into how being super connected all the time messes with teen girls' mental health. Sure, tech's great for a bunch of reasons, but there's a downside we can't ignore.

Imagine this: your day's filled with endless notifications, your eyes barely leaving the screen, and your brain trying to keep up with the endless online chatter. Sound like your life? Well, this chapter is all about hitting the pause button on that. It's time to chill out from all the digital buzz and focus on mental well-being.

We'll figure out why finding a good balance with our tech use is critical. Too much screen time? It messes with your sleep, can make you anxious or depressed, and even makes it hard to concentrate. But don't worry; we've got you covered with some solid tips on using your gadgets without letting them take over your life.

Next, we'll explore how to be more mindful and live in the moment. We'll try some exercises and tricks to help you calm your brain, reduce stress, and get to know yourself better. Plus, we'll see how getting back to nature, getting creative, and having face-to-face talks with people can make a huge difference.

So, if you're ready to take control and find peace in this wild, wired world, this chapter's for you. Let's learn how to tune out the noise, tune into ourselves, and create a healthier, happier mind.

RECOGNIZE THE INFLUENCE OF TECHNOLOGY

Tech's everywhere, right? Our phones, games, social media—it's like we're living online. But ever stop to think what that's doing to us? This chapter is about why too much screen time could be messing with our heads and how to deal with it.

First, let's talk about why zoning out on your phone or gaming for hours might not be so great. Have you ever felt down after scrolling through Instagram or TikTok for ages? That's because seeing all those "perfect" lives can make us feel like we're not measuring up. And it's not just about feeling low. Staring at screens all the time can mess up your sleep and make it hard to focus, too.

Now, how do you know if you're hooked on tech? Signs include feeling anxious when you're not checking your phone, ignoring real-life stuff to hang out online, and getting twitchy if you try to cut back. Notice yourself doing any of that? It may be time to rethink how you're using tech.

So, what can you do about it? Being the boss of your tech use is key. No phones at dinner or turning off screens an hour before bed. And remember, there's a whole world outside your screen. Getting active, diving into a hobby, or just chilling with friends and family can make you feel much better.

Wrapping it up, tech's cool, but it's all about how you use it. Too much can be a downer, but get the balance right, and you're golden. Pay attention to how tech's impacting you, set some boundaries, and make sure you're living your best life—both online and off.

RECOGNIZE SIGNS OF DIGITAL OVERLOAD AND ADDICTION

Tech's everywhere these days, right? It's like our phones and social media are glued to our hands. But have you ever thought about how all this screen time affects you? Technology addiction is a major problem and can result in serious side effects on your life. It's super important to understand how too much online can mess with our heads and what we can do about it.

First off, spending loads of time staring at screens makes us feel pretty bad about ourselves. Ever felt worse after scrolling through Instagram for hours? That's because comparing ourselves to others can make us feel like we're not good enough. And it's not just about feeling down. Too much screen time can also mess up our sleep, make us cranky, and even make it hard to focus on stuff. By taking note of these effects, you can reduce your screen time and prioritize activities that enhance mental wellness, such as engaging in outdoor activities, adopting hobbies, or talking to loved ones face-to-face.

Now, how do you know if you're getting too sucked into the digital world? Signs include:

- Feeling anxious when you're away from your phone.
- Frequently looking for your smartphone while eating your meals.
- Losing interest in your schoolwork or hobbies.
- Feeling a compulsive desire to go through your social media notifications.
- Feeling all jittery when you try to cut back.

If you're nodding along to this, it might be time to rethink how you're using tech.

So, what's the game plan? It's all about taking control of your tech use instead of letting it control you. Set some rules for yourself, like no phones during dinner or turning off screens before bed. Mix in some activities that don't involve screens, like getting outside, picking up a hobby, or just hanging out with family and friends. This can help you find a good balance between online and real life.

Getting a handle on your tech use is central to keeping your head in a good place. By being smart about screen time, recognizing when it's becoming a problem, and finding a healthy balance, you can make the most of tech without letting it mess with your mental and emotional well-being. Remember, it's all about using tech as a tool to make your life better, not letting it take over.

PRACTICE MINDFUL DIGITAL HABITS

In this super digital age, our whole lives seem to be online. But it's essential for us, especially teen girls, to get smart about how we use our tech. Let's talk about making some smart moves to keep our digital life healthy and positive.

First up, setting boundaries with tech is key. Imagine having certain times or places where you don't use your phone or computer. Like, when you're doing homework or hanging out with your family, you keep the screens off. And what about making your bedroom a no-phone zone at night? This can actually help you sleep better without all those notifications and blue light buzzing around. It's all about ensuring tech doesn't take over every part of your life.

Then, there's being mindful about what you do online. Instead of just endlessly scrolling or comparing yourself to every perfect pic you see, try to follow people or join groups that actually mean something to you. You know, where you can learn, share ideas, or just feel good about being you. And hey, why not spread some of that positivity yourself? Share things that inspire you, support causes you believe in, or make someone's day a little brighter.

Using tech to express yourself and grow is another terrific way to go. Whether it's writing, photography, or any other creative thing you're into, there are tons of digital tools out there to explore. Starting a blog or a vlog can be a great way to share your thoughts and experiences with others. Plus, so many online courses and tutorials can help you learn new skills and really dive into your interests.

So, being in this digital world has its challenges, but it's also full of opportunities. By setting some boundaries, choosing how you spend your time online wisely, and using tech to express yourself and learn new things, you can totally make your digital life work for you. Remember, it's all about finding that sweet spot where you're using tech in a way that feels good and right for you.

CONNECT WITH OTHERS AND TAKE CARE OF YOURSELF

In today's world, where we're all about likes, shares, and follows, it's super important to remember to connect with people face-to-face and take care of ourselves beyond the screen. Here's the lowdown on how to balance your online and offline life, keeping your mental health in check and finding joy in the little things.

First off, real-life connections matter a ton. Sure, social media is cool for meeting people and staying in touch, but nothing beats hanging out with your friends in person. Whether it's grabbing a coffee, going for a hike, or just chilling at the park, these real moments build stronger friendships than any online chat could. Make time for these hangouts; they're the good stuff in life.

Then, there's the whole self-care vibe. It's not just a trend; it's about ensuring you feel good inside and out. This means doing stuff that helps you chill and clear your head, like meditation, jour-naling, or just taking a long bath while your favorite tunes play in the background. It's about giving yourself a break and doing things that make you happy.

And remember to get your creative juices flowing! Diving into hobbies like painting, writing, or even baking can be very relaxing and a great way to express yourself. It's all about finding what you love to do and just going for it. Plus, it's a break from the endless scroll on your phone.

Balancing your life in this digital age can be challenging. Still, by focusing on real connections, taking care of your mental health, and getting creative, you can totally make it work. It's about enjoying the best of both worlds while keeping your well-being front and center.

HOW EMMA FOUND THE POSITIVE IMPACT OF OFFLINE CONNECTIONS

Emma Sommergill, a teen from Utah, found herself caught up in the digital whirlwind, feeling anxious and isolated due to constant screen time. But everything changed one afternoon when she dusted off an old board game. Inviting her friends over, they enjoyed a game night that sparked real laughter and conversations, something Emma realized she'd been missing amidst her online life.

Motivated by this experience, Emma sought out more real-world activities. She joined a yoga class, diving into practices that brought her peace away from the digital chaos. This wasn't just about physical fitness; it was a mental reset, teaching her to handle life's ups and downs with a calm mind.

Emma didn't stop there. She rediscovered the joy of reading, diving into books that offered her new perspectives and a break from the pressures of everyday life. These stories and characters became her guides, offering the insights and understanding she craved.

These changes sparked a significant shift in Emma. She grew more self-aware, learning to set boundaries for her well-being. Her transformation inspired her friends, who also started exploring their interests beyond the screen.

Emma's journey emphasizes the power of disconnecting and focusing on self-care. Her story calls us all to find balance in this digital age, reminding us of the importance of real connections and personal growth away from the glare of our devices.

COMING UP

In today's world, where everything is just a click away, it's easy for teen girls (or anyone) to feel caught up and overwhelmed. This chapter has been all about finding balance amid the chaos of constant notifications and online noise. It's about taking back control and finding peace within ourselves.

First off, setting boundaries with how we use tech is key. It's about choosing to pause, reflect, and do things that genuinely make us happy instead of mindlessly scrolling through social media. Imagine trading an hour of screen time for some quality time with a book or meditating. It's these moments of rest and self-reflection that safeguard our mental health from the endless digital buzz.

Then, there's the magic of real-life connections. Sure, texting and DMs are great, but nothing beats laughing with friends in person or hugging someone you care about. These natural, tangible experiences with people and nature ground us, offering a sense of support and belonging that no online interaction can match.

Now, as we gear up for the next chapter, we're diving into the game-changer: a positive mindset. It's about recognizing our inner strengths and using positive affirmations to boost our confidence. This isn't just feel-good advice; it's about building a foundation of resilience and self-esteem to help us tackle anything life throws our way.

So, let's get ready to explore how positive thinking can unlock our potential and lead us to a more fulfilled life. It's about finding that inner power and shining bright, even when the world feels a bit too much.

harness the power of a positive mindset

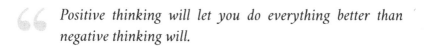

> *Positive thinking will let you do everything better than negative thinking will.*

— ZIG ZIGLAR

Imagine this: Inside you, there's this incredible power, like a superhero's strength. It's all about having a positive mindset. This means seeing the glass as half full, believing in yourself, and never giving up. It's like having a mental toolbox that's full of resilience and determination. And guess what? You'll learn how to tap into this superpower and use positive affirmations to change your life.

You know how sometimes the world tries to point out what's wrong with us? Well, real power doesn't come from what people think or say; it comes from inside you. Starting to think positively is like turning on a light in a dark room. It helps you see problems as chances to grow and to be the captain of your own ship.

This cool quote by Zig Ziglar hits the nail on the head for what this chapter is about. Your thoughts shape your world. If you think negatively, it's like building walls that stop you from doing great things. But with positive thinking, you can climb over any obstacle, see challenges as chances, and reach for the stars.

Positive affirmations are like your personal cheerleaders. They're short, powerful statements that encourage you to believe in yourself. They rewire your brain to think positively about who you are and what you can do.

By thinking positively, you open doors to new opportunities. You start to see things in a more hopeful and creative way. You become like a magnet for good stuff, attracting positive experiences and people who lift you up.

So, this chapter is all about discovering the amazing strengths you have inside. We will dive into how positive affirmations can totally revamp your mindset and help you achieve your dreams. Get ready to see how a positive mindset can bring out the best in you and lead to incredible results!

UNDERSTAND THE POWER OF THOUGHTS: UNLEASH YOUR INNER POTENTIAL

Our minds hold a remarkable power. They structure our emotions, impact our actions, and eventually define who we are. Do you realize that your thoughts and feelings can shape your world and who you are? It's like being on an epic quest to discover the best version of yourself, and it all starts with understanding how powerful your thoughts are.

Imagine waking up one morning feeling super tired and thinking, "Today's going to be awful." That kind of negative thought can totally color your whole day. But what if you flip that thought around and tell yourself, "I can handle whatever today throws at me"? Suddenly, you feel more positive and ready to take on the world.

We often don't realize how much our inner critic can hold us back. It's like this little voice inside that tells us we're not good enough or smart enough. But guess what? You've got the power to challenge those negative thoughts. Start by noticing when you're doubting yourself or being too critical. Ask yourself, "Is this really true, or am I just being hard on myself?"

Here's another example: Say you're stressing about a big test and thinking, "I'm never going to pass." Hold up and think about it for a second. Is that really true, or is it just fear talking? Remind yourself of the times you've done well and the effort you've put in. Swap out that negative thought for something more positive, like "I've worked hard, and I can do this."

Building a positive inner voice is like having your own personal cheerleader. It starts with positive affirmations—these are like little confidence boosts you can tell yourself to help change how you think. For example, saying "I deserve love and respect" or "I'm unique and confident" can help build self-esteem.

Your thoughts greatly impact how you feel and what you do. By focusing on the positive, you can change your whole vibe and outlook on life. And when you start this journey, remember you're strong enough to face any challenges. Believe in your mind's power—it's the key to unlocking your awesomeness.

STAY POSITIVE AND RESILIENT

Picture this: You're on an adventure. Along the way, you'll hit some tough spots – like people throwing shade or trying to bring you down. But don't sweat it because there are ways to skate through this and come out even stronger.

First things first, remember that haters and pressure from others don't define you. Those negative comments? They're more about the other person's issues than about you. Your real value? It comes from inside you. Build up your self-esteem like it's your superhero armor against all that negativity.

Next up, make sure you're hanging with a crowd that lifts you up. Find friends, mentors, or coaches who have your back. Look up to people like Greta Thunberg, a young environmental advocate who faced backlash for her environmental campaigns. Regardless of the negativity, Greta surrounded herself with a supportive network of fellow activists and fought for what she believed in, igniting a global movement for climate action.

Now, let's talk about handling criticism. It's not always easy but learning to tell the difference between helpful feedback and just plain mean comments is vital. Look at Misty Copeland – a fantastic dancer who didn't let negative talk about her body or race stop her. Misty is the first-ever African American principal dancer at the American Ballet Theatre. Throughout her dancing career, Misty confronted judgment about her body structure and race. Rather than allow it to frighten her, she channeled that effort into becoming a solid champion for inclusivity in the dance world, influencing countless others along the way. She used it to fuel her drive and opened doors for more diversity in ballet.

When someone's critiquing you, think about where they're coming from. Is it a legit concern, or are they just trying to knock you down? Keep the good stuff and ditch the rest. Remember, it's your choice who to listen to.

So, here's the deal: dealing with negativity and criticism is all about being resilient, surrounding yourself with good vibes, and learning how to grow from the tough stuff.

You've got to remember that you're more than what others say about you. Check out people like Greta and Misty – they're living proof that staying positive and using criticism to grow can lead to some awesome stuff. Trust in your journey, believe in yourself, and let your awesomeness shine, even when things get a bit cloudy.

EMBRACE GRATITUDE AND DEVELOP A POSITIVE MINDSET

Alright, check this out: Life can throw a bunch of curveballs, right? But guess what? This nifty trick called being grateful and optimistic can totally change the game. It's like having a secret power to turn a bad day into a better one.

First up, let's chat about being grateful. It's all about taking a second to notice and appreciate the good stuff in your life, no matter how small. It could be your friend's funny text, that fantastic sunset, or just chilling with your favorite music. When you focus on the good things, it's like a magnet for more good vibes.

Think about Oprah Winfrey. She had a tough start, but she got into writing down three things she was grateful for every day. And guess what? It totally transformed her life. It's like she flipped a switch and started attracting all this positivity. So, why not give it a try? Grab a notebook and jot down stuff you're thankful for. It's a game-changer, for real.

Now, let's talk optimism. It's like looking at a problem and saying, "Hey, I got this." Instead of getting stuck on what's going wrong, you see it as a chance to grow and learn. It's all about that positive mindset.

So, next time you're facing something challenging, flip the script. See it as a challenge you can totally handle. Remember, you've got the strength and smarts to get through anything and reach those big goals of yours. Keep that positive energy going; you'll be amazed at what you can do.

In a world full of problems and uncertainties, embracing gratitude and optimism can be helpful techniques to find a way through life's ups and downs. By showing gratitude, developing optimism, and making good use of visualization techniques, you can establish a positive mindset that uplifts you to embrace the present and manifest your dreams. Let's make an effort to dig deeper into these strategies and get a better understanding of how they can improve your well-being.

To start with, being grateful includes mindful appreciation of the present moment and acknowledging the blessings in your life. Take a brief moment to reflect on all the things you are thankful for, big or small. It could be the helping hand of loved ones, the wonders of nature, or even the simple happiness of everyday life. By shifting your focus to gratitude, you attract positivity and satisfaction into your heart.

It is fitting to look at the story of Oprah Winfrey, who, despite facing many obstacles in her early years, embraced a practice of gratitude. Oprah's daily practice of journaling three things she was grateful for helped her maintain a positive outlook and invite more blessings into her life—and her life improved exponentially. This practice can motivate you to find joy and acknowledge the abundance surrounding you.

Developing optimism is also essential to help you embrace a positive mindset. It includes redefining problems as opportunities for development and learning. Rather than dwell on drawbacks, approach them with an optimistic perspective. Believe that you have the power and resilience to get over obstacles and accomplish your goals.

Picture this: Bethany Hamilton, an excellent surfer, had a major setback when a shark attack cost her an arm. But guess what? She didn't let that stop her. Instead of backing down, she charged ahead with a super positive attitude. She learned how to surf with just one arm and totally rocked it. Bethany became a huge inspiration, showing everyone you can overcome tough stuff and still chase your dreams.

Now, let's talk about a cool trick called visualization. It's like daydreaming with a purpose. Close your eyes for a second and picture yourself nailing your goals. Imagine every detail—the feelings, the success, everything. Doing this helps align your brain and actions with what you want. It's like giving yourself a mental roadmap to where you want to go. So, next time you aim for something big, take a moment to visualize it happening. You'll be surprised how much it can help you get there!

HOW AISHA AND LEENA TRANSFORMED THEIR LIVES THROUGH GRATITUDE AND OPTIMISM

In the rural countryside of Georgia, two young girls, Aisha and Leena, embarked on remarkable journeys of self-discovery, transformed by the fantastic forces of gratitude and optimism. Despite growing up in a small, struggling family, Aisha, a dream-filled young girl, always found comfort in the beauty of nature around her. Instead of giving in to despair, she sat by the river each evening, reflecting on the blessings in her life. Aisha showed her gratitude by tending to her family's garden, growing vibrant flowers that proved her unwavering appreciation. Her positive outlook not only brought joy to her own life but also inspired her neighbors to find beauty in simple things.

Leena, a tough and determined girl, bravely confronted challenges with a strong will. She didn't let negativity bring her down, choosing optimism as her guiding force. Inspired by stories of regular people accomplishing amazing things, Leena believed in the strength of positivity. Motivated by this belief, she set out on a mission to uplift her community.

Leena arranged workshops for less privileged children, educating them about gratitude and planting seeds of hope for a brighter tomorrow. Her positive outlook transformed her life and sparked resilience in those around her. Through her actions, Leena became a source of inspiration and strength for the people she reached.

Fate brought Aisha and Leena together at a local community center, where they realized their shared values. Recognizing their potential as a united force, they decided to create a ripple effect of positivity in their town. Through a gratitude festival, they inspired many to adopt grateful and optimistic attitudes, turning their town into a hub of positivity and resilience.

Aisha's and Leena's inspiring journey spread far and wide, becoming a source of inspiration for people in surrounding towns. Their narrative shows the extraordinary power of gratitude and optimism. It can remind everyone that, no matter how challenging circumstances may be, gratitude can reveal inner beauty, and positivity can guide one towards a brighter tomorrow. Embrace the lessons learned, embark on transformative paths, infuse life with gratitude and optimism, and contribute to a world where joy and hope flourish.

COMING UP

In the highs and lows of your journey, you can tap into your inner strength, courage, and willpower. Embrace your natural abilities like self-belief, perseverance, and adaptability to overcome seemingly tough challenges. You can rise above self-doubt and embrace your unique qualities, finding peace in your inner wisdom.

Embarking on a journey of personal growth opens the door to the strength of positive affirmations. When you purposefully read encouraging statements, you transform your mindset and reconsider your beliefs. With each affirmation that acknowledges your value, utilizes your skills, and fosters self-compassion, you reinforce your inner strength, creating a path toward a satisfying and meaningful life.

Let your journey inspire you to embrace your strengths, respect your unique qualities, and affirm your true value. Recognize the transformative power of positive affirmations, aligning your thoughts with your highest capabilities.

As you move forward, remember that tapping into your inner strength and positive affirmations is an ongoing journey. With commitment and perseverance, you can have a life full of purpose, resilience, and lasting happiness. In the next chapter, explore the concepts of resilience and determination.

CHAPTER 7

grow your optimism with personal pep talks

 Believe you can and you're halfway there.

— THEODORE ROOSEVELT

We begin this chapter with the story of Rhoda, a girl from New York who grew up with not much money but a lot of hope. Even when things were tough, she kept aiming for big things in school, sports, and her community.

Rhoda didn't let hard times stop her. Instead, she used her problems as a chance to learn and be creative. She'd sit by her window every morning, look at the stars, and tell herself positive things. This helped her believe in herself.

She was a very positive person and helped her friends feel the same way, especially when things were hard. Rhoda's story shows how important it is for teenage girls to think positively and believe in themselves.

This chapter discusses why positive thinking is good for you and how you can make positive sayings that fit your life. It's all about helping girls be strong, believe in themselves, and grow. By thinking positively and saying good things about yourself, you can better deal with being a teenager, be more confident, and take control of your future.

FOSTER A POSITIVE MINDSET

Building a positive attitude is like training your brain to see tough times as chances to learn and improve. It's about keeping faith in yourself, even when things get complicated. Try to hang out with positive and supportive people and talk openly about your feelings and ideas. This can really change the way you look at things. Remember, when you face a problem, it's just a bump in the road, not a measure of what you can do. Getting through tough times makes you stronger.

Make sure to celebrate even the little wins. This helps you feel more confident and positive. Realize that your thoughts have a lot of power. If you start looking at problems as opportunities, you'll gradually become more positive, even when things are tough.

Here are some strategies to help you on this optimism journey:

- **Gratitude practice:** Keep a gratitude journal to jot down things you're thankful for daily or weekly.
- **Positive reframing:** Train the mind to turn negative thoughts into positive ones, focusing on solutions rather than problems.
- **Goal-setting:** Set achievable goals, both short-term and long-term, and celebrate each milestone achieved.
- **Mindfulness and meditation:** Practice mindfulness exercises to reduce stress and promote a positive mindset.

- **Build a support network:** Surround yourself with supportive friends, family, or mentors who uplift and encourage you.
- **Self-compassion:** Practice being kind to oneself during difficult times, embracing imperfections, and learning from setbacks.
- **Seek help:** Encourage seeking guidance from trusted adults, teachers, or counselors when facing challenges.
- **Engage in positive activities:** Participate in hobbies, sports, or activities that bring joy and fulfillment.
- **Limit negative influences:** Reduce exposure to negative media or situations that can impact your optimism.
- **Learn from adversity:** Embrace challenges as opportunities for growth and learning rather than viewing them solely as obstacles.

When practiced regularly, these strategies help build and sustain a more optimistic outlook on life.

Silver Linings and How to Find Them in Challenges

A "silver lining" is like finding a glimmer of hope in a dark cloud. When life gets tough, it's about spotting something positive even in challenges. You know the saying, "Every cloud has a silver lining"? Well, it means that even when things are hard, there's something good waiting to be discovered. For example, you go to softball camp and find that your best friend is not in your group. But you meet other girls in your group and make new friends with them.

Being a teenager can feel like you're on a crazy rollercoaster of emotions and challenges. But there's a way to find the good in tough times, and it can actually make you stronger. Here's how:

- **Change How You See Problems**: Instead of seeing problems as just bad things, try to view them as opportunities to learn and grow. This can help you build a powerful mindset.
- **Build a Support System**: It's super helpful to have people you trust, like friends, family, or mentors, to talk to. They offer different perspectives and can help you find new ways to tackle your problems.
- **Be Kind to Yourself**: Remember, figuring out who you are is a big part of being a teenager. It's okay to make mistakes – they're just part of learning. Don't be too hard on yourself.
- **Practice Mindfulness**: Doing things like meditation, writing in a journal, or getting creative can be really calming. These activities help clear your mind, which is great when you're facing challenges.
- **Grow Your Mindset**: Believe you can improve and grow with effort and hard work. This kind of mindset will give you the strength to face challenges head-on.

These tips are not just about getting through tough times; they're about finding hope and growing stronger from each challenge. They're great tools to help you get through your teenage years with confidence and power.

A Growth Mindset and What it Does for You

Having a growth mindset is really important for thinking positively. It means believing you can improve at anything if you work hard, practice a lot, and learn from when things don't go right. Instead of just getting praised for what you achieve, it's better to get praised for your effort. This way, you'll see that improving and making progress is more valuable than being perfect.

Here's what a growth mindset does for you:

- **Helps You Believe in Your Abilities**: Know that you can improve your skills and intelligence with hard work and practice.
- **Helps You Learn from Mistakes**: Understand that making mistakes is a part of learning and getting better.
- **Helps you Value Effort Over Perfection**: Realize that trying hard and making progress is more important than being perfect.
- **Helps You Set Realistic Goals**: Make goals that you can actually achieve. Break them into smaller steps so they're easier to manage.
- **Helps You Celebrate Small Wins**: Recognize and feel good about every small improvement you make.

How Do I Get a Growth Mindset?

Getting a growth mindset is key to doing better in life. Think about "not yet" instead of "can't do it" to change your view on your abilities. Realize that hard work and effort are more important than being naturally good at something. Skills grow with practice and determination.

Here's how you can develop a growth mindset:

- **Set Goals**: Make goals that are tough but reachable. They help you become stronger. When you face a challenging situation, see it as a chance to learn and grow.
- **Learn from Failures**: Think of failures as steps to get better, not dead ends. This will improve your problem-solving skills and make you more confident.
- **Reflect on Yourself**: Regularly check your progress and

look for ways to improve. Celebrate every bit of progress to remind yourself that you're always getting better.

- **Look Up to Role Models**: Pay attention to stories of people who succeeded through hard work. Their journeys show how a growth mindset can lead to success.
- **Create a Supportive Space**: Be in an environment where it's okay to make mistakes. Focus on learning rather than being perfect. Be curious, try new things, and follow your interests.

By doing these things, you'll be more ready to take on challenges and reach your highest potential.

BUILD AFFIRMATIVE HABITS

Creating good habits is a great way to feel stronger and improve your well-being. This includes practicing positive self-talk, using affirmations to boost your confidence, and being thankful for what you have. These habits help build your self-confidence and make you more resilient.

Positive self-talk is super important. It means talking to yourself in a kind and encouraging way. If you are too hard on yourself, try to change those thoughts to something positive. For example, if you think, "I can't do this," change it to, "I'll try my best." By repeating positive phrases like "I am capable," "I deserve happiness," or "I am enough," you start to believe in yourself more. This helps change the way you think and makes you feel more empowered.

Boost Your Confidence with Daily Positive Statements

Creating your own affirmations that match what you want to achieve and who you would like to be helps build good habits. Think about the areas in your life where you want to grow and make positive statements about these areas. Saying things like "I am confident in my abilities," "I embrace my uniqueness," or "I am deserving of success" can really lift your spirits and make you see yourself in a good light. When you make these affirmations, focus on what you're good at and what you hope to achieve, and keep a positive attitude about it all. Here are some examples:

- "I can achieve my goals through hard work and dedication."
- "My potential is limitless, and I am worthy of success."
- "I embrace challenges as opportunities for growth and learning."
- "I trust myself to make decisions that align with my values and dreams."
- "I am resilient and overcome obstacles with courage and determination."
- "My unique qualities and talents make a positive difference in the world."
- "I deserve happiness, love, and respect, and I attract positivity into my life."
- "I am confident in my abilities and believe in my capacity to create change."
- "I am enough just as I am and continually grow into a stronger version of myself."
- "I am in control of my thoughts and actions, shaping my destiny."

Using affirmations specific to your goals and aspirations can boost your self-esteem and reinforce a positive self-image. Focus on what you're good at and what you hope to achieve and keep a positive attitude about it all.

Develop a Habit of Gratitude and Appreciation

Practicing gratitude every day can really improve your life. Start each day by thinking about what you're thankful for. This helps create a positive mindset where you focus more on what you have instead of what you don't. Write down a few things you're grateful for to grow your appreciation for the little and big things in life.

Saying thank you to others, either by words or small actions, is also important. This builds empathy and strengthens your relationships, creating a happier and more supportive environment. To stay mindful, you can practice being grateful during regular activities, like meals or before you go to bed. Reflecting on the good parts of your day can help you see the positive side of challenging situations, making you more resilient and optimistic.

Doing kind things for others can increase the benefits of being grateful. You could volunteer, help someone out, or do something nice unexpectedly. This not only makes you feel good but also enables you to make a positive impact on others. Making gratitude a regular part of your life helps you notice and appreciate the good things more, leading to a happier mindset, stronger relationships, and better overall well-being.

Setting aside time each day to think about what you're grateful for, like your friends, what you've achieved, or even small everyday joys, can shift your focus to the good in your life. This builds a feeling of contentment and strength. Positive self-talk, empowering affirmations, and a habit of gratitude can boost your confidence, help you grow as a person, and lead to a happier, more satisfying life.

PUT POSITIVITY INTO ACTION

Turning positive thoughts into real-life actions can really change your life for the better. This means making your everyday actions positive and finding ways to add positivity to your daily routine.

Start each day with a clear plan. Decide to be positive from the moment you wake up. This could mean setting goals for the day, being thankful for what you have, or doing things that make you feel good, like hobbies or self-care activities.

To make your positive thoughts real:

- Do nice things for yourself and others.
- Treat yourself well by doing things that are good for your mind, body, and soul, like being mindful, doing hobbies you love, or taking care of yourself.
- Spread positivity to others by helping a friend, doing volunteer work, or just complimenting someone.

Remember, even small steps can lead to a happier life. Work little by little towards your dreams and goals. This could be learning something new, spending time on personal growth, or following your passions. Doing a bit every day will make you feel accomplished and lead you to a more positive, fulfilling life.

Stir Positivity into Relationships

Adding positivity to your relationships can really change your life for the better. Being positive doesn't just make you feel good, but it also strengthens your relationships with your family, friends, and classmates.

When you're positive in your relationships, you show more empathy, kindness, and understanding. This helps you connect better with the people you care about, making your relationships more meaningful. Being positive also means you're better at handling disagreements and problems in a way that's healthy and keeps the peace.

Building positive relationships means really talking and listening to each other. Show that you appreciate and understand how the other person feels. This builds trust and makes your relationships stronger. It's also important to forgive and let go of hard feelings, which allows your relationships to grow.

Celebrate what's good about the people around you. Give them genuine compliments and support to make them feel good, too. Little acts of kindness or even just a nice word can make your relationships stronger.

Setting boundaries is important, too. You need to take care of yourself and make your needs clear. Respecting each other's boundaries builds trust and respect.

Being positive with your classmates is essential as well. Create a friendly and welcoming atmosphere by respecting everyone's differences, standing up against negativity, and being kind and understanding. This way, you and your friends support and encourage each other.

Extend Positivity Beyond Your Personal Boundaries

In a world that often emphasizes self-centeredness and negativity, the power of positivity should never be underestimated. As a teen girl, you possess incredible potential to extend positivity beyond your personal boundaries, creating a ripple effect that can transform your communities and even reach wider society. By understanding the impact of your actions and embracing acts of kindness and support, you can become a catalyst for positive change.

Let's look at the following points:

- **The ripple effect of positivity on the community and beyond:** Positivity has the remarkable ability to spread and multiply like ripples in a pond. When you radiate positivity, it influences those around you, creating a domino effect that can reach far beyond your immediate circles. By nurturing a positive mindset and engaging in uplifting behaviors, you inspire others to do the same. This ripple effect can uplift entire communities, fostering unity, resilience, and a sense of well-being.
- **The power of contributing to a positive environment:** You can shape the environment in which you live. By actively contributing to a positive atmosphere, you create welcoming, inclusive, and supportive spaces. Acts of kindness, empathy, and respect can transform schools, social groups, and online communities, creating an environment where everyone feels valued and empowered. By championing positivity, you become a leader who inspires others to follow suit.
- **Acts of kindness and support as tools for change:** Small acts of kindness and support can have a meaningful impact on individuals and the wider society. You can make a difference by reaching out to those in need, offering a helping hand, or lending a listening ear. By showing compassion, understanding, and support, you create a network of encouragement and resilience that uplifts those around you. These acts of kindness not only improve the lives of others but also strengthen your own sense of purpose and fulfillment.

You possess incredible potential to extend positivity beyond your personal boundaries, becoming an agent of change in your community and beyond. Through the ripple effect of positivity, you can create a domino effect that transforms the world around you. By embracing acts of kindness and support, you contribute to a positive environment that nurtures and empowers everyone.

Blend Positive Affirmations into Daily Activities

In today's world, where people often focus on themselves and see the negative side of things, being positive is very powerful. As a teenage girl, you have an amazing ability to spread positivity beyond just your own life. Your actions and kindness can really make a difference in your community and the wider world.

Here's how your positivity makes a difference-

- **You Spread Positivity Far and Wide**: Just as ripples spread across a pond, your positive attitude can spread to others. When you're positive, you influence the people around you, and this can keep spreading outwards. Maintaining a positive attitude and doing positive things can inspire others to do the same. This can bring a lot of good vibes to entire communities, making them stronger and happier.
- **You Create a Positive Space Around You**: You can shape the world you live in. Being positive makes the places you go, like school or online spaces, welcoming and kind. Simple things like being kind, understanding, and respectful can improve these spaces. This way, everyone feels valued and supported.
- **You Use Kindness and Support as Tools for Change**: Small acts of kindness can mean a lot. You can help others by listening to them, offering support, or just being there when they need someone. This not only helps others but also makes you feel good and purposeful. Your kindness

can strengthen your community and spread good vibes all around.

Extending positivity and kindness beyond yourself can really change things for the better in your community and beyond. Your positive actions can start a chain reaction, transforming the world around you. By being kind and supportive, you help create a better environment for everyone.

How Teens Can Overcome Negativity

Life often throws you challenges, testing how tough and positive you can be. You can use some handy strategies and a strong, resilient mindset to handle these tough times and stay positive. Let's look into ways to deal with life's hurdles and keep a positive attitude.

Handling Challenges While Staying Positive

Staying positive when things get tough takes real effort. Start by accepting your feelings, even the negative ones. It's okay to feel down sometimes. Then, focus on the good things in your life, like what you're thankful for. Doing things that make you feel good, like exercising, practicing mindfulness, or enjoying your hobbies, can help manage stress and keep you in a good mood. Talking to friends, family, or mentors you trust can also give you a big boost.

Overcoming Setbacks with Resilience

Everyone faces setbacks, but it's how you deal with them that matters. Think of these challenges as chances to learn and grow, not just roadblocks. Having a growth mindset means seeing tough times as steps toward your goals. Break big goals into smaller, more manageable ones to keep your spirits up. Being kind to yourself and saying positive things in your mind can help you bounce back stronger after a setback.

Dealing with challenges and staying positive can be challenging. Yet, with resilience and the right mindset, you can get through tough times. Use gratitude, self-care, and support from others as tools to help you. Remember, setbacks can be chances to learn and grow.

NORAH AND THE POWER OF POSITIVE THINKING

Norah, a high school student in California, had her ups and downs just like any other teenager. But she stood out because she really believed in thinking positively.

When Norah had to face a big math test, a subject that always troubled her, she started to doubt herself. With the test getting closer, she felt more and more anxious. But Norah didn't let these negative thoughts win. She knew her way of thinking could really change her situation.

In the days before the test, Norah constantly told herself positive things. She believed she was smart and could do well in math. She even pictured herself acing the test and feeling proud.

On test day, Norah went in feeling confident. Every time a doubt popped up while she was taking the test, she pushed it away with a positive thought. She trusted in her abilities, and it showed in her work.

When the test results came out, Norah was nervous. To her surprise, she didn't just pass; she got the top score in her class! Her positive thinking really worked wonders.

This experience was a game-changer for Norah. She realized that positive thinking wasn't just a nice idea but a powerful tool to face any challenge. From then on, she kept a positive attitude in everything she did.

Norah's story quickly spread around her school. Her friends and classmates were inspired by her and started to think positively, seeing how it could change their lives.

Norah's story teaches us that with a positive mindset, we can get through tough times, reach our goals, and make our futures brighter. Her journey shows us the real power of positive thinking.

COMING UP

In this part of the book, you've learned the importance of having a positive attitude and using affirmations for your well-being and personal growth. By keeping a positive mindset, you start to believe in what you can do and find ways to get past tough times. You also discovered how making positive habits, like saying good things to yourself every day and thinking positively, can really boost how powerful you feel.

When you act on positive thoughts, you're taking real steps toward your goals.

This makes you stronger, boosts your confidence, and helps you discover your purpose. In this chapter, we learned that maintaining a positive attitude and using affirmations equips you to handle life's ups and downs. It's all about growth and unlocking your true potential. And guess what? In chapter 8, we'll dive into building resilience and determination- bouncing back when life knocks you down.

develop resilience and determination

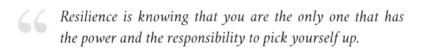
> *Resilience is knowing that you are the only one that has the power and the responsibility to pick yourself up.*
>
> — MARY HOLLOWAY

Think of resilience like a river that keeps flowing, no matter what blocks its way. It twists and turns, dodges rocks, and cuts through landscapes, always moving forward. That river is a lot like us as we face life's challenges, showing us how to keep going and adapt, no matter what.

Resilience is what helps people get back up after life knocks them down. It's not something you're born with, but you can definitely build it up, like a muscle, with practice and effort.

Being a teenager is tough. You're going to run into all sorts of challenges that test how strong you are. But don't worry—you've got what it takes to get through tough times. Inside you, there's an incredible strength waiting to tackle any problem head-on and win. By learning about resilience and determination, you're setting yourself up to navigate life's ups and downs. This part of your life is about discovering how to be resilient and filled with the drive to keep moving forward, no matter what.

Do you wonder why it is so important to know about resilience? Resilience matters because it is the starting point. It's not about avoiding problems or pretending everything's fine when it's not. It's about knowing deep down that you have what it takes to tackle these problems head-on. Think of challenges as your personal trainers, making you stronger and wiser with each hurdle you jump over.

HOW TO BUILD RESILIENCE AGAINST CHALLENGES

Here are some techniques that can help teens build resilience. Many of these will seem like common sense, and that you've heard them before. But, consciously reviewing these hints and remembering to use them will make a difference.

- **Get enough sleep:** Getting enough sleep is essential for maintaining good physical and mental health. It can help you feel more alert, focused, and energized, which can help you cope with stress and adversity.
- **Stay connected with others:** Having supportive relationships with family, friends, and peers can help you feel more connected and less isolated. It can also provide a sense of belonging and help you build a support network.
- **Set and achieve goals:** Setting and achieving goals can help you build confidence and a sense of accomplishment. It can also help you stay motivated and focused on the future.
- **Express your emotions creatively:** Expressing your feelings through creative outlets such as writing, art, or

music can help you process difficult emotions and reduce stress.

- **Take time out to relax:** Taking time out to relax and engage in activities you enjoy can help you recharge and reduce stress. This can include activities such as reading, listening to music, or spending time in nature.

Remember, building resilience takes time and effort, but it's worth it. By practicing these techniques, you can find your inner strength and develop the skills and mindset needed to overcome life's challenges. Focus on the things you can control instead of being stuck on what you cannot change.

BEING RESILIENT IS EASIER WHEN YOU KNOW HOW TO ADAPT

You become adaptable by strengthening your problem-solving skills.

Boosting your bounce-back game means being like water— flowing with whatever comes your way. Life's gonna throw some curveballs, and the trick is to swing back by being flexible. Dive into new experiences, check things out from a fresh perspective, and don't shy away from stepping into the unknown. That's your secret weapon to getting comfy with changes and leveling up your challenge-crushing skills. Plus, becoming a problem-solving pro is a massive boost to your resilience. It's all about learning to navigate the ups and downs smoothly.

So, how does one strengthen one's problem-solving skills?

- **Identify the problem**: The first step in problem-solving is to identify the problem. What do you think the problem is, and where is it coming from?
- **Think about why it's a problem**. See if you can answer some of these questions: Why is this so important to you? Why do you need this? What do you think might happen? What's upsetting you? What's the worst thing that could happen?
- **Brainstorm possible solutions to the problem**: It's essential to consider all options, even if they seem unrealistic or silly.
- **Evaluate the options**: After brainstorming, evaluate each option. Think about the pros and cons of each solution.
- **Create a plan to move forward**: Once a solution has been chosen, create a plan to move forward. You may need to break the plan down into smaller steps and set realistic goals.
- **Practice, practice, practice**: Problem-solving is a skill that takes practice, so look to practice problem-solving in everyday situations.
- **Stay positive**: This will help you stay motivated and focused on finding a solution.
- **Take pride in your small steps.** You may not find a solution right away.
- **Use your calming skills**: Remember deep breathing, meditation, or yoga. This is a perfect time to use these skills.

DEVELOP DETERMINATION

Determination is the quality of being firm and resolute in pursuing a goal or objective. It involves having strong willpower and an unwavering focus on the end result.

Here are some strategies you can use to help you stay firm in your determination:

- **Set SMART goals**: Set goals that are Specific, Measurable, Achievable, Relevant, and Time-bound. This will help you to stay focused and motivated.
- **Break goals down into smaller steps**: This will make it easier for you to stay on track and not feel overwhelmed.
- **Create a plan for achieving your goals.** : This should include a timeline, items you'll need, and thoughts on what you will do if something gets in your way.
- **Stay organized**: Use a planner or calendar to keep track of your goals and progress. This will help you stay focused and motivated.
- **Celebrate successes**: Celebrate your successes along the way. This will help you stay motivated and feel good about your progress.
- **Stay positive**: Keep your vibes up and look on the bright side! This will help you stay focused even when the going gets a bit tough.
- **Practice problem-solving skills**: This will help overcome barriers and stay focused on the goal.
- **Stay accountable**: Sharing your goals with others can help you stay on track and committed to reaching your goals.
- **Stay flexible**: Adjust your goals if needed and look for other ways you could meet your goals if you start to feel

stuck. This will help you avoid feeling discouraged if things don't go according to the original plan.

Remember, maintaining determination is all about staying focused and motivated, even when things get tough. By practicing these strategies, you can develop the skills and mindset needed to achieve your goals.

WHAT IS PERSEVERANCE ALL ABOUT?

So, you know how sometimes life throws stuff at us that feels just too much? Like the time you sprained your ankle while playing tennis? Your recovery from that injury required resilience, but it also needed perseverance. You may have had daily therapy, icing, using crutches as you struggled through the pain. Perseverance is about sticking to your goals and not giving up, even when things get tough. Here's the lowdown on how you can be all about that perseverance life:

- **Dream Big but Start Small:** Make goals that you can actually reach. It feels incredible to check something off your list, and it's all about taking steps that get you closer to where you want to be.
- **Believe in Your Power to Grow:** Understand that you can get better at pretty much anything if you put your mind and effort into it. Messing up doesn't mean you're not capable; it's just a step in the learning process.
- **Be Your Own Role Model:** Show some grit in what you do. Talk to others about your own challenges and how you didn't let them stop you. It's about showing that if you can do it, anyone can.
- **Got Your Back:** Be there with a hug or a high five to celebrate the small victories and offer a shoulder when

things aren't going right. Support makes everything
easier.

- **Problem-Solving Queen:** When you're faced with a
  problem, break it down into pieces you can handle. Look
  at it from different angles and come up with ways to
  tackle it.
- **Cheers to You:** Recognize all the hard work you put in and
  the progress you make, no matter how small. It's about the
  journey, not just the destination.
- **Bounce Back Like a Boss:** Encourage facing challenges
  head-on and learning from slip-ups. It's all about getting
  up, dusting yourself off, and going at it again, stronger
  than before.

By weaving these tricks into your life, you're not just surviving;
you're thriving. It's about building that stick-to-it spirit that helps
you crush it, no matter what life throws your way. Ready to
conquer the world?

WHAT DOES "EMPOWERING RESILIENCE" REALLY MEAN FOR TEEN GIRLS?

Empowering resilience means finding your inner strength and
using it to face challenges head-on. It's about believing in yourself
and trusting your abilities, even when things get tough. It's also
about embracing your unique qualities and talents and not letting
setbacks define you. You're capable of adapting to change and
bouncing back from tough times. Confidence is key, and it's okay
to ask for help when you need it. Building resilience against negative comments and societal pressures involves fostering self-confidence, setting boundaries, and seeking supportive networks. It
also requires embracing imperfections, practicing mindfulness,
and developing critical thinking skills to challenge societal norms."

Remember, resilience is all about finding your inner strength and using it to overcome life's challenges.

To stay positive, it's important to avoid negative people and places. Instead, focus on building a circle of positive influences. This means surrounding yourself with people who support you and help you grow. It also means creating an environment that encourages your personal development and well-being. Remember, staying positive is all about surrounding yourself with positivity and avoiding negativity.

Develop Resilience Against Negativity and Social Pressures

Think of resilience as a superhero against negativity and pressure. It's about boosting your self-belief, knowing when to say, "enough is enough," and hanging out with people who lift you up, not drag you down. It means loving your quirks, staying cool and present in the moment, and not just accepting what everyone else thinks without questioning it. Resilience is your secret power to bounce back from tough times.

Always make sure you're looking after yourself and staying in a good headspace. If things get too much because of bad vibes around you, don't hesitate to chat with someone you really trust or get help from a pro. You have every right to be in a place that makes you feel good and supported.

A STORY ABOUT RESILIENCE AND DETERMINATION

In a bustling Minnesota city filled with dreamers, there was a girl named Eva who was a force to be reckoned with. Facing challenges that seemed too tough to beat, Eva never let the city outshine her spirit. She had big dreams of being her own boss, creating stunning jewelry from stuff most people would throw away, all from the corner of her small apartment.

Getting her jewelry out there took a lot of work. She faced a lot of "no's" when she tried to get a spot at the local market to showcase her work. But Eva didn't give up. She kept tweaking her designs and talking to the people in charge until one kind soul gave her a shot.

Eva's booth quickly stood out, drawing crowds with her unique, eye-catching creations. Her pieces weren't just jewelry; they were symbols of never giving up, crafted with heart and fierce determination.

Soon, everyone was talking about Eva's work, making her a local celebrity and a source of inspiration for other young dreamers. She proved that with enough grit, you can turn your dreams into reality, no matter how many hurdles you face.

Eva's journey shows that true success starts with believing in yourself and never backing down, lighting the way for others to follow their passions.

COMING UP

Life's like climbing a massive mountain. It stands for all the hard stuff you'll face, from tricky tests to bad days. To reach the top, you need a mix of resilience, determination, and perseverance. Think of resilience as your safety gear against the tough spots; it helps you stand up again after a fall. Determination is that inner force driving you upwards, focused on the win. And perseverance? That's your will to keep going, even when the finish line feels a million miles away.

Every challenge is part of the journey up. Being resilient means you're set for these challenges, ready to bounce back and find ways through the tough times. It's about turning every obstacle into a chance to grow stronger. Determination keeps your eyes on the goal, even through the mist, and perseverance means you don't quit, no matter what.

By sticking to resilience and determination, you're arming yourself to face anything life throws at you. It's not just about reaching the top but learning along the way. Your journey is similar. Keep at it, remain steadfast and driven, and no peak is too high. In Chapter 9, you'll learn about hormonal imbalances and how they affect teenage girls.

CHAPTER 9

hormonal imbalance and teenage girls

> *You should be at your most powerful when you're going through your weakest moments.*
>
> — C. JOYBELL

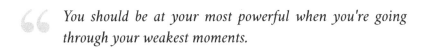

eing a teenager is like being on a rollercoaster of emotions, thanks to hormone changes. It's like what C. JoyBell wisely noted about being strong even when things get tough. This is super important as you face all the ups and downs of growing up. Hormones can make you feel all over the place—happy one moment and totally not the next. Think of the resilience you need to navigate the hormonal fluctuations that dominate your teen years (Goodreads, n.d.). Hormones affect how you feel about yourself, how you get along with others, and even your health.

This part of the book is about understanding what messes with your hormones, how it makes you feel and look, and how to keep things balanced. It's also about knowing when you might need to ask for help if things feel too out of control. Hormones like estrogen and progesterone are key players in your body, especially for girls. They keep your periods regular and affect your mood. But when they're out of whack, things can get messy, like getting your period at random times, breaking out, gaining weight, or mood swings.

I want to share a story about my sister, Linda, who really struggled during her teen years. She went from being super happy to crying in no time, all because of her hormones. She also started breaking out and pulling back from hanging out with friends. Luckily, we got help from a doctor who taught Linda how to deal with these changes—like eating right, staying active, and finding ways to chill out. It made a huge difference.

Linda's story shows how important it is to get the scoop on hormones and how they affect you. Knowing what's going on and getting the right support can help you ride out this crazy time with your head held high.

UNDERSTAND HORMONAL IMBALANCE

When you're a teenager, your body's basically on a huge transformation spree, moving you from kid to adult. This journey involves several hormones, like estrogen and progesterone, which are super important for many things your body does. But sometimes, these hormone levels can get out of whack, and that's what we call hormonal imbalance. For teen girls, this imbalance can mess with your emotions and body in a bunch of ways, changing how you feel day-to-day and overall messing with your vibe.

Common Causes of Hormonal Fluctuations During Adolescence

A lot of things can make your hormones go wild. When you hit puberty, your body starts pumping out hormones. This is what kicks off changes like your period starting, your breasts growing, and pubic hair coming in. But it's not just puberty—your genes, how you live your life, the stress you're under, and even where you are can mess with your hormone levels. If you're not eating right, skipping workouts, or not getting enough sleep, that can also throw your hormones out of balance.

How to Identify Hormonal Imbalance

Getting why your hormones are out of balance is essential in dealing with it. If your periods are all over the place, you're breaking out, gaining weight, feeling moody, easily annoyed, always tired, or even super down or anxious; these could be signs. These things can hit differently for everyone and mess with your day-to-day and how you feel about yourself.

Understanding what's up with your hormones helps you take charge of your health. Learning more about it, getting help from doctors when you need it, and looking after yourself can assist you in getting through these changes stronger and ready to tackle any hormone-related hurdles.

UNDERSTAND THE EMOTIONAL EFFECTS OF HORMONAL IMBALANCES

During your teen years, hormones like estrogen and progesterone go on a rollercoaster, which can mess with your feelings. You might find yourself swinging from super happy to really annoyed or sensitive without much warning. One minute, you're chill, and the next, you're not, which can be confusing and tricky to handle.

Understanding how these hormonal ups and downs play with your emotions is crucial. Hormones aren't just about physical changes; they also control the brain's chemicals that influence how you feel and react to things. When your hormones are all over the place, it can throw off these brain chemicals, leading to mood swings or feeling out of sorts. The hormone changes are messing with the brain's wiring, affecting how you see things and react in different situations.

A Story of Emotional Challenges Due to Hormonal Imbalances

Camila's story is a great example of how hormonal changes can play a significant role in a teenager's emotional health. Just like Camila, you might find your mood flipping from super happy to really down or angry in no time, and it can be confusing not just for you but for people around you, too. Camila learned that her mood swings were because of hormonal imbalances, which are common during teenage years.

With the right help, Camila found ways to deal with these emotional ups and downs. She started using mindfulness techniques, exercising more, focusing on self-care, and getting support from her family and friends. These steps helped her manage her feelings and feel more in control.

If you're going through something similar, remember Camila's story. Understanding the connection between your hormones and how you feel is the first step. Then, with the right strategies and support, you can handle the emotional rollercoaster of your teen years much better, just like Camila did.

UNDERSTAND THE PHYSICAL AND HEALTH EFFECTS OF
HORMONAL IMBALANCES

When you're going through your teen years, your body's
hormones can be all over the place, showing up in a few different
ways. One common thing a lot of teens face is acne. This happens
because your body makes more oil, blocking your pores and
leading to breakouts. Your weight might also change—it could go
up, or you might find it hard to keep weight on. These changes can
make you feel different about how you look, which can be pretty
tough on your confidence and how you feel inside.

But it's not just about what you can see on the outside. These
hormone shifts can mess with your periods, making them irreg-
ular or really painful. They can even lead to issues like polycystic
ovary syndrome (PCOS), which affects your ovaries and can cause
problems with your menstrual cycle and fertility down the line. It's
really important to talk to a doctor if you're noticing these changes
so you can get the right advice and support.

**How Other Teen Girls Coped With the Physical and Health
Impacts of Hormones**

Grace, a 16-year-old from Miami, went through a tough time with
hormonal imbalances that caused severe acne, making her feel
really down about herself and less keen on hanging out with
friends. She decided to get help from a skin doctor, who helped
her find the proper skincare routine. Over time, her skin cleared
up, and she felt way better about herself.

Then there's Lucy from Washington, who had problems with her
periods being all over the place and really painful. She got advice
from her doctor and started using hormonal birth control to make
her periods more regular and less painful. This helped her keep up
with school and her hobbies without any trouble.

Dealing with hormonal imbalances isn't just about the physical stuff; it's also about taking care of your health in general. Getting the right medical advice, living a healthy lifestyle, and finding treatments that work for you are all steps you can take to manage these changes. It's all about making sure you're feeling good during these years of significant changes.

Strategies to Manage Hormonal Imbalances Effectively

Going through your teen years means dealing with lots of mood swings because of hormone changes. It's super important to take care of yourself during this time. Exercising, getting plenty of sleep, and eating right can help keep your hormones in check. Also, doing things that chill you out, like meditating, writing down your thoughts, or getting into your favorite hobbies, can make you feel more relaxed and happier overall.

Having ways to deal with challenging feelings is vital. Try breathing deeply, chatting with someone you trust, or getting creative with things like art, music, or writing to let out what you're feeling. Being able to understand and share your emotions in a good way can lower your stress and make you feel better emotionally.

THE IMPORTANCE OF SEEKING SUPPORT FROM HEALTHCARE PROFESSIONALS

When you're dealing with hormone issues, getting help from medical pros like doctors or gynecologists is super important. They know the ins and outs of what's going on with your body and can give you the right advice or treatment you might need. They can figure out why you're feeling off, come up with a plan to help you feel better, and answer any questions about the changes you're going through.

Seeing a therapist could also be a big help. They can support you emotionally through these confusing times, helping you deal with feelings and situations that come up because of hormone changes.

Talking openly with these healthcare experts is key. Don't be shy about sharing what you're feeling or noticing about your body. Asking questions is a good thing—it means you're taking charge of your health. Remember, these people are here to support you and make sure you stay healthy, both in your body and your mind, as you go through these changes.

Encouraging Words for You to Embrace Your Body and Emotions at This Time of Change

Being a teenager means you're going to see a lot of changes in your body and feelings. It's super important to be kind to yourself instead of trying to match up to impossible standards. Remember, everyone's journey is different, and it's okay to look and feel different from others. Doing things that make you feel good about yourself, like hanging out with friends who support you, choosing to watch or read stuff that makes you feel positive, and reminding yourself of your worth, can really boost how you feel about yourself.

Your emotions might feel all over the place during these years, and that's totally normal. It's okay to lean on friends, family, or even a counselor when things get tough. They can be your go-to people for advice or even when you need to "vent."

Embracing who you are, finding ways to deal with stress, and getting advice from doctors when needed can help you overcome the ups and downs of growing up. This time in your life is about learning more about who you are and building the skills you'll use for the rest of your life.

Take Violet's story, for example. She's a 13-year-old from Hawaii who started noticing changes because of hormone shifts. Some days, she felt super sad for no reason, and other times, she couldn't stop laughing or crying. Thanks to her friend Brittany and her mom, she realized she wasn't alone. They encouraged her to talk to a doctor, who helped her understand what was happening and assured her she had support. At the doctor's office, Violet met Dr. Anderson, a kind and empathetic healthcare professional. Dr. Anderson explained that hormonal imbalances during adolescence were common and could show up in various ways. She assured Violet that she was there to help navigate this change.

Dr. Anderson gave Violet some awesome tips to deal with the hormone rollercoaster. She stressed how important it is to look after yourself by getting enough sleep, eating right, and staying active. Violet also picked up some cool, stress-busting hobbies like journaling and sketching her thoughts and feelings.

Over time, Violet figured out what worked best for her. Taking long walks in the park helped clear her head, and writing in her journal became a safe space for her to spill her thoughts without worry. These methods really helped her feel more in tune with her emotions.

Despite the challenges, with support from her family, friends, and doctors, Violet learned to accept and love her changing body and emotions. She realized her worth wasn't tied to her hormone levels but to her ability to bounce back and find her inner strength.

Violet even started to spread the word about mental health and self-care at school, setting up workshops to talk about dealing with teenage troubles and how to handle hormone shifts. Her story encouraged others to get help and look at life's changes in a positive light.

Looking back, Violet saw how facing her hormone issues head-on made her not just stronger but also kinder and more understanding. She felt ready for whatever life had in store next, armed with confidence and a whole lot of heart.

Like Violet, reaching out for help and talking about what you're going through is a big step towards feeling better and more in control of your life during these changing times.

COMING UP

Getting why your hormones are all over the place is super important for keeping up with self-love and feeling powerful. When you get what's happening with your body and emotions during these changes, you can figure out the best ways to deal with it all. Being kind and understanding to yourself is crucial when you're riding the hormone rollercoaster.

Knowing about the stuff like off-schedule periods and feeling super tired helps you find the right way to handle it. Talking openly, taking good care of yourself, and sometimes even chatting with doctors can assist you in getting through these changes and feeling strong and positive.

This journey is all about growing into your confidence and learning to love yourself every step of the way. And guess what? Chapter 10 will dive even deeper into how you can rock this whole self-love and empowerment thing.

CHAPTER 10

Sustaining self-love and empowerment

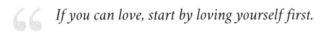

> *If you can love, start by loving yourself first.*

— CHARLES BUKOWSKI

C harles Bukowski starts this chapter by reminding us how crucial it is to love ourselves. Before you can connect with others, you must begin with loving yourself. Then, we dive into accepting and celebrating who you are. It's about silencing that voice inside that criticizes you and replacing it with kindness and understanding. Recognizing your worth is a big step in this life-long journey of self-love. We'll explore how doing good things for your mind, body, and soul helps keep self-love strong. Also, setting boundaries and having friends who respect them is vital.

You'll learn about the importance of speaking up for yourself and recognizing what you're good at. We'll use real stories and examples to show you how to be bold and stand up for yourself and others. We read about people who've faced tough times and how they got through them, teaching you about bouncing back, adapting, and believing in yourself. Think of challenges as chances to grow and learn how to face anything that comes your way with confidence.

Lastly, we all know that life throws challenges our way, but bouncing back from them is what builds our strength and resilience. You'll read about people who've faced tough times and how they got through them, teaching you about bouncing back, adapting, and believing in yourself. Think of challenges as chances to grow and learn how to face anything that comes your way with confidence.

NURTURE SELF-LOVE

Let's chat next about how you, as a teen girl, can really embrace self-love. It's all about finding ways to feel good about who you are. You can start by writing in a journal, using positive affirmations, and practicing mindfulness. These are terrific ways to get to know yourself better and stay positive.

Doing stuff you love, caring for yourself, and hanging out with friends who support you are super important. They help keep your self-love tank full.

Self-acceptance and being kind to yourself are essential, too. It means being okay with not being perfect, recognizing what you're good at, and giving yourself a break. It's about switching off that negative voice in your head and treating yourself with the same kindness you'd show a friend.

Dealing with tough times is part of the journey. Developing a growth mindset means seeing challenges as chances to learn and get better. Seeking advice from people you trust, like mentors, friends, or therapists, can really help when things get rough. Building resilience, setting achievable goals, and celebrating your successes, no matter how small, also make a big difference.

Remember, self-love is a continuous journey. By sticking with these practices, accepting yourself, and pushing through the hard stuff, you're building a solid base of self-love. This will empower you to face life's challenges confidently and genuinely appreciate your own unique awesomeness.

CONTINUE TO EMPOWER YOURSELF

Now, let's talk about how you can keep growing and feeling great about yourself. It's like going on an adventure where you're the hero of your own story.

Start by setting cool goals for yourself. These could be anything from getting better grades to learning a new hobby. When you chase after these goals, you're stepping outside your comfort zone. This is where you grow and discover what you're capable of.

Life can throw some curveballs, but guess what? That's actually a good thing. When you start seeing challenges as chances to learn something new, you begin to grow a 'growth mindset.' This means you're ready to adapt and change, no matter what comes your way.

Building resilience is super important, too. Think of it as your secret superpower that helps you bounce back when things get tough. You can do this by taking care of yourself, managing stress like a pro, and having people around who've got your back.

So, by embracing change, tackling new challenges, and looking after yourself, you're on the path to keep growing and being the best version of yourself. It's all about using your inner strength to overcome obstacles and live a happy, empowered life. Keep going, and you'll see how amazing you can be!

How to Keep Your Empowerment Journey Alive and Growing

Sustained self-love is the pillar of ongoing encouragement for you. By developing a deep feeling of love and acceptance for yourself, you unlock your potential and embrace your unique qualities. Believing in yourself is a gift. It pushes you to tackle tough stuff, follow your dreams, and keep feeling good about your life. It's all about knowing you can handle whatever comes your way and going after what you want, making your life awesome in the process!

Inspiring Stories of Personal Empowerment

Name: Lorna

Age: 17

Background: Lorna grew up in a place where everyone expected girls to follow old-fashioned rules and not stand out too much. But Lorna was different. She wasn't about to let those old ideas stop her. She loved music and dreamed of starting her own band. So, Lorona did just that, breaking the mold of what people thought she should be. Sure, she got some side-eyes and had to deal with people doubting her, but Lorna didn't give up. Her band became her way of speaking up, showing that girls can rock just as hard, and inspiring others to chase what they love. Lorna's journey taught her, and everyone watching, that being true to who you are and following your dreams is what really matters.

Name: Jillian

Age: 16

Background: Jillian, a teenager, had a tough time dealing with bullies and people making her feel bad about her body. But instead of letting it get her down, she decided to do something about it. She started practicing mindfulness and caring for herself, finding a special connection with yoga and meditation. These activities helped her feel calm and in control. Jillian even began sharing her experiences on social media, inspiring others. She created a community where everyone celebrated loving themselves and their bodies just the way they are. Jillian's story shows how taking care of yourself can change your life and help you be proud of who you are.

Name: Trudy

Age: 18

Background: Trudy was really into helping the environment and making sure the planet stayed healthy. She didn't just talk about it; she actually did stuff! She organized things like recycling programs, got people together to plant trees, and taught others how important it is to live in a way that's good for the Earth. Trudy's hard work and excitement about the environment got other kids her age to join in. They even started a group run by young people to keep making positive changes for the environment. Trudy's actions showed everyone how powerful it is when people work together for a cause they believe in and how even one person can make a big difference in the world.

Name: Isabella

Age: 15

Background: Isabella had a tough time because people expected her to look a certain way, which was messing with how she felt about herself. But she didn't let that stop her. She got help from someone who could guide her and joined a group that was all about loving yourself and being okay with how you look. Isabella worked hard on being kinder to herself, doing things that made her feel good, and thinking positively. As she started feeling better about who she was, she decided to help others. She talked about how important it is to be cool with your body and care for your mind. Isabella's story helped many other girls learn to love themselves just as they are.

Name: Olivia

Age: 16

Background: Olivia really cared about making things fair and right for everyone. She didn't just talk about it; she did stuff to make a difference. She helped out in her community, worked with local groups, and got people talking about important issues. Her hard work and passion got other teens excited, too. They all came together and started their own group focused on social justice. Together, they spread the word, held protests, and worked to make changes. Olivia showed everyone that if you're really into something and work with others, you can make a big impact and help yourself grow at the same time.

Personal Stories Supporting Ongoing Self-Love and Empowerment

Theresa, who's 17 and lives in the busy streets of New Jersey, had a tough time with how she saw herself. She'd put on some weight and was dealing with acne, which really knocked down her self-esteem. But Theresa didn't let this get her down for long. She started going to therapy and spent time thinking about who she was and what she wanted. This led her to start loving herself more. She decided to share her journey on a blog, talking honestly about her struggles and what she learned. This wasn't just for her, though; she wanted to help others who felt the same way. Theresa became a big supporter of being positive about your body and caring for your mental health. She encouraged everyone to be cool with who they are and to appreciate their own kind of beauty. Her story ended up inspiring a lot of other girls to look after themselves better and to really embrace who they are.

Maud, who's 16 and lives in Maryland, Virginia, really loves art. But when she told her friends she wanted to be an artist, they weren't very supportive. Instead of getting upset, Maud decided to do something about it. She set up her own website to show off her art. On this site, she talked about how art was a way to express herself. This website turned into a fantastic place where other young artists could share their art and be themselves without worrying about what others thought. Maud's efforts showed other young artists that it's okay to be creative, to stop worrying about what people think, and to use their passion to find happiness and confidence.

Lila, who's 15 and lives in California, had a tough time at school because she was bullied a lot. But she didn't just accept it; she decided to do something about it. She started a group at her school to fight against bullying. They met regularly to support each other and talk about how to deal with bullying. Lila put together activities like workshops and school assemblies to teach everyone about how harmful bullying can be. She also ran campaigns to spread the word about being kind and understanding each other. Thanks to her hard work, students who were bullied felt braver to speak up, and even those who weren't directly affected learned to be more accepting and kind. Lila's efforts helped create a friendlier and more loving atmosphere at her school.

Sharon, who's 17 and lives in Georgia, is really into protecting the environment and making the world a better place. She started a fantastic project called "Green Generation" to get people in her area to care more about environmental issues. She organized things like recycling drives, cleaning up the neighborhood, and teaching others about how to live more sustainably. Sharon wanted everyone, especially other young girls, to get involved and see that they could make a big difference in taking care of our planet. Her work has been all about showing people that they can be environmental heroes in their own way.

Sophie, at 16 years old, became a champion for LGBTQ+ rights in Alaska. Understanding how important it is for everyone to feel accepted, she set up a GSA club at her school. This club became a place where LGBTQ+ students and their friends could hang out, share their stories, and support each other. Sophie organized all kinds of activities like workshops, talks from guest speakers, and campaigns to help everyone at her school learn about and embrace diversity. Her efforts helped many students, especially girls, to be proud of who they are, appreciate the diversity around them, and stand up for equal treatment and inclusivity in every part of life.

COMING UP

To grow as a person and feel good about yourself, it's super important to love and accept who you are. Taking care of yourself, being okay with your flaws, and speaking kindly to yourself are the keys to building this self-love. Also, to really empower yourself, keep challenging yourself, setting goals, and trying new things. Remember, the people around you matter a lot! Having friends, mentors, and role models who support you can help keep you motivated and feeling strong. When you love yourself, you're more ready to face tough times, chase your dreams, and succeed in whatever you do. Now, how do you keep that positivity alive and well in your life?

a respectful request

I hope you enjoyed reading this guide and that you came away with some ideas that you can use right now in your life. If you think this book will help other teens, please take a few minutes to share your positive thoughts on this book by leaving a review on Amazon. You may have found several "glimmers" or ideas that you hadn't thought of before. One can only imagine the difference that can be made by sharing these thoughts with your friends and with your family

Reviews are important to any author, especially those of us who are independent.

Even if it's only a sentence or two, it will be helpful to other readers as well as to me.

Click on this QR code to leave your review now:

Thank you.

keeping life's positivity alive

Before we go any further, I want you to know that I have included an extra chapter for this book. It's for parents, guardians, grandparents, mentors, and other role models in your life to read. This journey is tough enough to go through and it's important for you to have the understanding and support of others. Please share this book with them, especially the next chapter. Having a few adults on your team makes this journey easier.

As we wrap up this incredible journey, let's think about what C. JoyBell said: "I'm the only one who can bring me down, and I'm not going to let myself do that anymore." This quote is all about loving yourself, which is a big theme we've talked about in this book, made just for girls like you.

The biggest takeaway is that you have all the power inside you. Nobody else can decide how much you're worth or how you should feel about yourself. You've got this amazing ability to shape your own life and how you see yourself. Learning to love yourself means you don't need others to tell you you're good enough; it's all about believing in yourself, bouncing back from tough times, and being emotionally healthy.

In the first chapter, we talked about how knowing yourself really well is the first step to truly loving yourself. We tried out things like paying close attention to our thoughts and feelings, writing in journals, and taking time to think about our lives.

Chapter 2 was all about believing in yourself and learning ways to boost your confidence, like setting goals you can actually reach, celebrating the little wins, and pushing yourself to try new things.

In Chapter 3, we looked at how to feel more balanced and healthy. We learned about managing stress, taking care of ourselves, and making sure we have a good balance between work and play.

Chapter 4 taught us to appreciate how unique our bodies are and to think positively about how we look, by accepting everyone's differences, being kind to ourselves, and not buying into what society says is beautiful.

Chapter 5 talked about the importance of stepping away from screens and focusing on our mental health, through managing how much time we spend online, making meaningful friendships, and practicing self-care.

In Chapter 6, we discovered how powerful positive thinking and believing in growth can be. We discussed how the way we talk to ourselves can make a huge difference, how to be resilient, and how to recognize our own strengths.

Chapter 7 was all about the power of a positive mindset, changing the way we think to be more positive, and the magic of telling ourselves we're capable and valuable.

Chapter 8 showed us that setbacks are part of life, but we also learned ways to come back even stronger. We covered how to deal with tough times and when it's okay to ask for help.

Chapter 9 focused on the challenges teenage girls face, like the changes during puberty and how they affect our mood and self-esteem. Understanding and getting support through these changes can help us be kinder to ourselves, bounce back from difficulties, and feel empowered.

Chapter 10 stressed the need to keep caring for ourselves and to keep empowering ourselves. We learned ways to maintain a good relationship with ourselves, set boundaries, and improve our emotional health.

Throughout this book, we've emphasized how crucial self-love, confidence, resilience, and emotional wellness are for leading a fulfilling life. By embracing these qualities, you'll spread positivity, build healthy relationships, follow your dreams fearlessly, overcome challenges with grace, and embark on a lifelong journey of loving yourself. Always remember that you're worthy, capable, and deserving of love and happiness.

As we bring this book to an end, I hope you don't put it on your shelf, never to look at it again. If you are serious about taking control of your life, you may want to revisit specific chapters to refresh your spirit and remind yourself of important strategies you learned. Hold onto the words of C. JoyBell as a reminder that you have the power to lift yourself up. The world is waiting to see your light shine, and I'm confident that with self-love, confidence, resilience, and emotional well-being, you'll achieve great things and make a positive impact!

Best wishes.

CHAPTER 11

how you can best support teen girls

THE CHAPTER FOR PARENTS,
GUARDIANS, AND OTHER ROLE
MODELS-

> *Just when the caterpillar thought the world was ending, she became a butterfly.*
>
> — BARBRA HAINES HOWETT

Hello, parents, guardians, grandparents, and other role models. Do you realize how important you are to your teens? Just when they become more challenging to talk to, more difficult to understand, and dare I say it, more difficult at times to even like, is when they need you the most. Teens are full of hormones- their bodies and moods are changing, most times without their being aware of it. The quote above may be something for you to hang on to as you go through trying times with your teen, but it may be something to remind your teen about as well.

As a woman who was once a teenage girl, as the mother of 2 daughters who went through their teenage years, as the grandmother of 3 teenage granddaughters, and as a former 7th-grade teacher who worked with dozens of teen girls each school day, I'd like to share some tips that I wish I had known many years ago when I was raising my own daughters. These tips are on what this special group of teens needs most from you during their teen years.

You most likely purchased this book for your teen; however, it is vital that you not only know what they will be reading about in this book but also understand some of the key words and concepts.

If you haven't done so, please look at the table of contents. You will see many of the buzz words surrounding this topic. These are words such as resilience, positive mindset, perseverance, self-care, and others. In order for us, as well as your teens, to be on the same page (pardon the pun), I will share the definitions of these words as they will be used in this book

Finally, don't get too worried about the difficult times that you are approaching or are already in the midst of, for after all, as English poet Edward Fitzgerald once said, "This too shall pass."

KEY WORDS

Determination- is the quality of being firm and resolute in pursuing a goal or objective. It involves having strong willpower and an unwavering focus on the end result.

Empowerment-the process of becoming stronger and more confident, especially in controlling one's life and claiming one's rights

Mindfulness- the practice of being fully present in the moment, paying attention to your thoughts, feelings, and sensations without judgment. It helps reduce stress, improve mental well-being, and enhance focus and self-awareness.

Overwhelm- a state of being overwhelmed or inundated, completely defeated

Perseverance- continued effort to do or achieve something despite difficulty or delay in achieving success.

Positive mindset- a way of approaching life's challenges with a positive outlook. It does not mean one avoids or ignores bad things but instead makes the most out of bad situations, finds the best in other people, or sees oneself in a positive light. It does not necessarily mean avoiding or ignoring the bad things; instead, it involves making the most of the potentially bad situations, trying to see the best in other people, and viewing yourself and your abilities in a positive light.

Resilience- the ability to bounce back from challenging situations. It's about adapting well in the face of adversity, trauma, tragedy, threats, or sources of stress. This can include anything from family and relationship problems to serious health issues or workplace and financial stressors. It's not just about "getting through" challenges but also growing and potentially finding positive outcomes in difficult times. Resilience involves mental, emotional, and sometimes physical stamina that helps you handle difficult experiences and, in many cases, emerge stronger from them.

Self-love- the regard for one's own well-being and happiness (chiefly considered a desirable rather than narcissistic characteristic). Self-love is about loving yourself in a healthy way. It is knowing that we are flawed, yet we care about ourselves despite our imperfections. Self-love doesn't mean you don't care about others. Rather, it means being as kind to yourself as you are to others. Accept yourself fully, treat yourself with kindness and respect, and nurture your growth and well-being.

With these key terms defined, the hope is that you will better understand what the rest of this chapter is about.

WHY DO WE NEED TO LOVE OURSELVES?

If you grew up without any models for self-love or anyone who talked to you about the importance of being good to yourself, you might question its value.

Without self-love, you're likely to be highly self-critical and fall into people-pleasing and perfectionism. You're more likely to tolerate abuse or mistreatment from others. You may neglect your own needs and feelings because you don't value yourself. You may self-sabotage or make decisions that aren't in your own best interest.

Self-love is the foundation that allows us to be assertive, set boundaries and create healthy relationships with others, practice self-care, pursue our interests and goals, and feel proud of who we are.

SELF-LOVE VS. NARCISSISM

In addition to questioning whether self-love is really necessary, another significant barrier to self-love is the belief that it's narcissistic or selfish.

When psychologists and therapists encourage self-love, they aren't talking about putting yourself on a pedestal above everyone else. Narcissists believe they're better than others and won't acknowledge or take responsibility for their mistakes and flaws. They also seek extraneous amounts of external validation and recognition. Narcissists also lack empathy for others.

Self-love, on the other hand, isn't about showing off how great you are. People who love themselves in a healthy way know that they are flawed and make mistakes. They accept and care about themselves despite their imperfections. Self-love doesn't prevent you from caring about others; it simply means you can give yourself the same kindness you give others.

HOW TO NURTURE PERSEVERANCE IN YOUR TEEN

Encouraging and nurturing perseverance involves providing a supportive environment, teaching valuable skills, and demonstrating the importance of resilience in overcoming obstacles.

Nurturing perseverance in teen girls involves fostering resilience, determination, and the ability to persist through challenges.

Here are strategies to help you support and encourage a teenager's ability to persevere:

- **Encourage a growth mindset**. Remind your teen that that abilities can be developed through dedication and hard work. Emphasize the value of effort and learning from mistakes rather than just focusing on innate talent. Tell them stories of times you messed up and stuck with the problem until it was resolved.
- **Show them role models.** Talk with your teens about who they see as role models. Have a conversation about why they chose that person. Share some of your role models, such as your parents or other community members, and why you decided to model your actions after theirs. Stories

of women who've overcome obstacles can motivate and encourage any young woman.

- **Support their passions.** Encourage your teen to pursue activities they are passionate about- art, music, sports, academics, etc. When your teen engages in these activities, they're developing perseverance to overcome challenges within those pursuits.
- **Teach them problem-solving skills.** This is crucial. Give them examples from your life. Encourage breaking down problems into manageable parts and exploring various solutions. Take your time coming to their rescue when they get stuck. Instead of doing the task for them, ask them what they might do and talk through it.
- **Celebrate effort, not just achievement**. Praise your teen's efforts, not just their achievements. No win is too small to celebrate. Acknowledge their zeal regardless of the result.
- **Provide a safe environment for failure.** Encourage taking risks and learning from failures. Create an environment where they see mistakes as opportunities for growth rather than sources of shame.
- **Help them set realistic and achievable goals**. Unrealistic expectations can lead to discouragement, while achievable goals can foster perseverance.
- **Teach coping strategies**. Equip girls with coping mechanisms to manage stress and setbacks. Techniques like mindfulness, deep breathing, or journaling can help navigate challenging situations.
- **Encourage support networks**. Foster connections with supportive peers, mentors, or family members and you. Having a solid support network can provide encouragement during difficult times.
- **Lead by example.** Demonstrate perseverance in your pursuits. Share stories about when you didn't get

something you thought you really wanted. Still, things ended up being better than you initially thought. Your actions and attitude toward challenges can serve as a powerful example for teens to emulate.

HELP YOUR TEEN DEVELOP A POSITIVE MINDSET

Helping your teen develop a positive, healthy mindset involves several proactive strategies to support their mental and emotional well-being:

- **Open Communication:** Establish a safe and open environment for communication, encouraging your teen to express their feelings and thoughts without judgment.
- **Model Positive Behavior:** Demonstrate positive behavior and mindset in your own life. Teens often learn by example, so your approach to challenges and self-care will influence them.
- **Encourage Positive Relationships:** Support your teen in building strong, healthy relationships with family and friends. Positive social interactions can significantly enhance their mental health.
- **Foster Resilience:** Help them develop coping strategies for dealing with setbacks and challenges. Encourage them to see failures as opportunities for growth.
- **Mindfulness and Stress Management:** Introduce practices such as meditation, yoga, or other mindfulness techniques to help manage stress.
- **Set Realistic Goals:** Encourage your teen to set achievable goals and recognize their achievements, which can boost confidence and motivation.

- **Promote Gratitude:** Encourage them to reflect on and appreciate the positive aspects of their lives, which can shift focus away from negative thoughts.

HELP YOUR TEEN DEVELOP RESILIENCE

To help teens develop resilience, several strategies can be effective:

- **Encourage Connection:** Foster strong, positive relationships with family and friends. This support network can provide encouragement and help teens navigate challenges.
- **Promote Healthy Risk-Taking:** Encourage teens to step out of their comfort zone, try new things, and take on challenges within a safe and supportive framework.
- **Teach Self-Care:** Emphasize the importance of looking after their physical and mental health through regular exercise, a healthy diet, sufficient sleep, and mindfulness or relaxation techniques.
- **Develop Problem-Solving Skills:** Help teens learn to identify problems, think through solutions, and take steps to resolve issues, building their confidence and independence.
- **Foster a Growth Mindset:** Encourage teens to see challenges as opportunities to learn and grow rather than insurmountable obstacles. Praise effort, persistence, and resilience over mere success.
- **Model Resilience:** Demonstrate how to cope with stress and adversity in a healthy way. Teens often learn by example, so showing them how you navigate difficulties can be very instructive.
- **Encourage Emotional Intelligence:** Help teens understand and manage their emotions. Recognizing and

expressing feelings in a healthy manner is a critical
component of resilience.

- **Provide Opportunities for Reflection:** Encourage teens
  to reflect on their experiences, including failures, to
  identify what they learned and how they can apply those
  lessons in the future.

See what I mean about the key words? They are intertwined
within these concepts to the point that you can only talk about one
while using another. I hope that through reading this Parents'
chapter, you have a better understanding of the concepts in this
book.

Best wishes as you navigate the teen years with your teen and
remember to Enjoy the Journey!

a respectful request

Parents, Guardians, Grandparents, Mentors, Other Important Adults- I hope you enjoyed reading this special chapter and that you came away with some ideas that you can use right now in your life. If you think this book will help other families of teens, please take a few minutes to share your positive thoughts on this book by leaving a review on Amazon.

Your review is a source of insight and recommendation to others looking for this type of resource for their teen. The spirit of promoting self-love for teen girls stays alive when we share our knowledge and experiences.

Reviews are important to any author, especially those of us who are independent.

Even if it's only a sentence or two, it will be helpful to other readers as well as to me.

Click on this QR code to leave your review now:

Thank you.

references

Ackerman, C. E. (2019, May 29). *What is self-love and why is it so important?* Psych Central.

Alcedo, M. (2019, February 27). *20+ Quotes about Strength to Comfort You during Hard Times.* Country Living. https://www.countryliving.com/life/g5054/quotes-about-strength/

Cherry, K. (2021, May 3). *Resilience: Meaning, types, causes, and how to develop it.* Verywell Mind.

Drew, C. (2023, July 16). *27 Perseverance Examples.* Helpful Professor

Goodreads. *A quote by C. Joybell C.* Www.goodreads.com. Retrieved January 26, 2024, from https://www.goodreads.com/quotes/469248-choose-your-battles-wisely-after-all-life-isn-t-measured-by

Goodreads. (2019). *C. Joybell C. quotes (author of the sun is snowing).* Goodreads.com. https://www.goodreads.com/author/quotes/4114218.C_JoyBell_C_

Harris, K. (2022). *Amazon.com - life skills for teenage girls - google search.* Www.google.com. https://www.google.com/search?q=amazon.com+-+Life+Skills+For+Teenage+Girls&oq=amazon.com+-+Life+Skills+For+Teenage+Girls&gs_lcrp=EgZjaHJvbWUyBggAEEUYOdIBCDMxODFqMGo0qAIAsAIA&sourceid=chrome&ie=UTF-8

Inspiremykids. (2015, July 30). *35 Inspiring Quotes for Kids about Being Different and Being Yourself.* InspireMyKids. https://inspiremykids.com/35-inspiring--for-kids-about-being-different-and-being-your self/#:~:text=%E2%80%9CBe%20yourself.

Jacobson, S. (2017). *Confidence.* The Meaningful Life Center. https://www.meaningfullife.com/landing_page/confidence/?gad_source=1&gclid=

Kiusalaas, M. (2018, February 26). *Free the girl: A story about (finding) self-love by maya kiusalaas.* The Merit Club. https://www.themeritclub.com/new-blog-1/2018/2/15/free-the-girl-a-story-about-finding-self-love-by-maya-kiusalaas

Lee, E. H. (2022, February 24). *Resilience: 5 ways to help children and teens learn it.* Harvard Health Publishing.

Mills, A. (2023). *How to Recognize and Nurture Your Hidden Talents.* Www.google.com. https://www.google.com/amp/s/www.alden-mills.com/blog/how-to-recognize-and-nurture-your-hidden-talents%3fhs_amp=true

Nemours TeensHealth. (2023). *How can I improve my self-esteem? (for teens) - nemours kidshealth.* Kidshealth.org. https://kidshealth.org/en/teens/self-esteem. html#:~:text=Accept%20your%20best%20and%20let

Positive Psychology. (2023, October 13). *Positive Mindset: How to Develop a Positive Mental Attitude.* PositivePsychology.com.

Prasad, A. (2015, November 28). *8 steps for embracing your uniqueness - dr. asha prasad.* Dr Asha. https://drashaprasad.com/self-awareness/embrace-your-uniqueness/

Raising Children Network. (2021, November 5). *Problem-solving steps: pre-teens and teenagers.* https://raisingchildren.net.au/pre-teens/behaviour/encouraging-good-behaviour/problem-solving-steps

Sharpe, R. (2021, December 23). *150+ Self Love Quotes to Increase Your Self Esteem.* Declutter the Mind. https://declutterthemind.com/blog/self-love-quotes/

Tal Gur. (2023, May 7). *Calm mind brings inner and self-confidence, so that's very important for good health.* Elevate Society. https://elevatesociety.com/calm-mind-brings-inner-strength/

The Counseling Teacher. (2021, June). 100 Self-confidence boosting positive affirmations for students. The Counseling Teacher. https://thecounselingteacher. com/2021/06/100-self-confidence-boosting-positive-affirmations-for-students.html

Waters, B. (2013). *25 ways to boost resilience | psychology today.* Www.psychologytoday.com. https://www.psychologytoday.com/us/blog/design-your-path/201305/25-ways-boost-

Zig Ziglar Quotes. (n.d.). BrainyQuote. https://www.brainyquote.com/quotes/ zig_ziglar_125675

Made in the USA
Las Vegas, NV
17 December 2024

14534482R00075